HƆW
LEARNING WORKS

John Almarode | Douglas Fisher | Nancy Frey

HOW
LEARNING WORKS

a playbook

CORWIN

Fisher & Frey

FOR INFORMATION:

Corwin

A SAGE Company

2455 Teller Road

Thousand Oaks, California 91320

(800) 233–9936

www.corwin.com

SAGE Publications Ltd.

1 Oliver's Yard

55 City Road

London EC1Y 1SP

United Kingdom

SAGE Publications India Pvt. Ltd.

B 1/I 1 Mohan Cooperative Industrial Area

Mathura Road, New Delhi 110 044

India

SAGE Publications Asia-Pacific Pte. Ltd.

18 Cross Street #10–10/11/12

China Square Central

Singapore 048423

President: Mike Soules

Associate Vice President and
Editorial Director: Monica Eckman

Director and Publisher, Corwin
Classroom: Lisa Luedeke

Senior Content Development
Manager: Julie Nemer

Senior Editorial Assistant: Caroline Timmings

Editorial Assistant: Nancy Chung

Production Editor: Melanie Birdsall

Typesetter: C&M Digitals (P) Ltd.

Proofreader: Christine Dahlin

Cover Designer: Rose Storey

Marketing Manager: Deena Meyer

Printed in the United States of America

Library of Congress Cataloging-in-Publication Data

Names: Almarode, John, author. | Fisher, Douglas, author. | Frey, Nancy, author.

Title: How learning works : a playbook / John Almarode, Douglas Fisher, Nancy Frey.

Description: Thousand Oaks, California : Corwin, [2022] | Includes bibliographical references and index.

Identifiers: LCCN 2021026979 | ISBN 9781071856635 (spiral bound) | ISBN 9781071856666 (epub) | ISBN 9781071856659 (epub) | ISBN 9781071856642 (pdf)

Subjects: LCSH: Learning. | Learning strategies. | Motivation in education. | Effective teaching.

Classification: LCC LB1060 .A455 2022 | DDC 370.15/23—dc23

LC record available at https://lccn.loc.gov/2021026979

This book is printed on acid-free paper.

21 22 23 24 25 10 9 8 7 6 5 4 3 2 1

Contents

Visit the companion website at
resources.corwin.com/howlearningworks
for resources.

Note From the Publisher: The authors have provided video and web content throughout the book that is available to you through QR (quick response) codes. To read a QR code, you must have a smartphone or tablet with a camera. We recommend that you download a QR code reader app that is made specifically for your phone or tablet brand.

Acknowledgments

Corwin gratefully acknowledges the contributions of the following reviewers:

Dr. Lynn Angus Ramos
K–12 English Language Arts Coordinator
DeKalb County School District

Amy Colton
Education Consultant
Center for Collaborative Inquiry

Introduction

This playbook is about how learning works—not by chance, but by design. How do students learn and how can we leverage this knowledge into great learning, through the design of our classrooms, learning experiences, and tasks? We want our students to effectively learn the content, skills, and understandings associated with the specific subject area of focus. From inferences in English language arts, deforestation in environmental science, perspective in art, or spatial awareness in physical education, the range of topics and ideas is as diverse as the students in our classrooms. In addition, the content, skills, and understandings associated with each content area are not isolated from social, emotional, affective, and language learning. The characterization of learning as "reading, writing, and arithmetic" does not even come close to conceptualizing the highly complex, multidimensional, highly coveted outcome we strive for in our classrooms: flexible, durable, and usable learning.

Consider the dynamic first-grade classroom of Rebecca Anderson, where her students are learning about equivalence. Here is how she has clarified and articulated the day's learning.

LEARNING INTENTION

Today I am learning about things that are equal.

For example, $17 - 5 = 16 - 4$

Today I am also learning the importance of explaining my mathematics thinking to my classmates.

SUCCESS CRITERIA

I will know I have learned it when

- I can describe what it means to be "equal" in mathematics.

- I can determine if two number sentences are equal.

- I can explain my thinking using different models.

In addition to what is *explicitly* shared through her learning intentions and success criteria, use the space on the next page to develop a list of what additional learning Ms. Anderson's students are expected to know, understand, and be able to do. We will get you started with an example.

1. Different models for showing equivalence

2.

3.

4.

5.

6.

7.

Ms. Anderson clearly articulates what her students are expected to know, understand, and be able to do in the learning intentions and success criteria. But her students are learning more than that. There are aspects of this learning experience not explicitly stated by Ms. Anderson. For example, students must learn what language is involved in a mathematical explanation, how to structure a mathematical explanation, the different models for explaining their thinking, as well as the social, emotional, and affective aspects of persisting in problem solving and interacting with their peers. In other words, the learning expectations of Ms. Anderson are far more complex and have greater depth and breadth than merely determining whether $17 - 5$ is or is not equal to $16 - 4$. And this is as it should be. The underlying point of this example is that learning is complex and multidimensional, and therefore the learning experiences should be designed as such and not left to chance. Let's look at another example.

Betty Dixon is using *The Giver* by Lois Lowry as the anchor text for the following standards (National Governors Association Center for Best Practices, Council of Chief State School Officers, 2010):

1. **CCSS.ELA-Literacy.RL.8.2.** Determine a theme or central idea of a text and analyze its development over the course of the text, including its relationship to the characters, setting, and plot; provide an objective summary of the text.

2. **CCSS.ELA-Literacy.RL.8.3.** Analyze how particular lines of dialogue or incidents in a story or drama propel the action, reveal aspects of a character, or provoke a decision.

3. **CCSS.ELA-Literacy.RL.8.4.** Determine the meaning of words and phrases as they are used in a text, including figurative and connotative meanings; analyze the impact of specific word choices on meaning and tone, including analogies or allusions to other texts.

4. **CCSS.ELA.W.8.3b.** Use narrative techniques, such as dialogue, pacing, description, and reflection, to develop experiences, events, and/or characters. (© Copyright 2010 National Governors Association Center for Best Practices and Council of Chief State School Officers. All rights reserved.)

In this particular example, our focus is not necessarily on the explicit or implied learning intentions and success criteria, but on the transfer of learning. Ms. Dixon wants her students to learn about theme as well as the ways in which dialogue and character actions propel the plot forward, figurative and connotative meanings of words and phrases, and narrative techniques used by the author. She wants her learners to transfer this learning to other texts and incorporate these literacy skills into their own independent reading. Again, this is complex, multidimensional, and requires the careful design of learning experiences that result in both the learning of these ideas and the transfer of this learning to new contexts.

These two scenarios capture exactly what we set out to do in this playbook. Knowing how learning works can help us design experiences that amplify our students' learning outcomes. In other words, how do students learn, and how does the answer to this question impact the decisions Ms. Anderson and Ms. Dixon make in designing the learning experiences for their students? Furthermore, how can an understanding of their own learning benefit our students as they progress toward independent learners?

THE PURPOSE OF THIS LEARNING PLAYBOOK

The purpose of this playbook is to take a closer look at how our students learn so that we can better design learning experiences that align with how learning works. This playbook will engage us in unpacking *the science of how we learn* and design learning experiences that *translate* the science of how we learn into *promising principles and practices*. This includes *implementing* instructional approaches and strategies that promote learning and, at the same time, *monitoring* our impact on student learning through generating and gathering evidence of that learning. Richard Mayer asserts that "if you want to help people learn, it would be useful for you to know something about how learning works" (2011, p. vii). The modules of this playbook will focus on expanding your understanding of how students learn and how to better utilize these ideas in the classroom through a process that places the teacher at the center of this work (see Figure I.1).

However, you likely noticed that the final component of great learning by design is strategy instruction. In this playbook, we will also explore how to better engage students in understanding how they learn and the tools that foster, nurture, and sustain their own learning. We want students to take an active role in their learning, selecting the most effective tools to move their own learning forward.

For a video introducing the purpose of the playbook, visit the companion website at resources.corwin.com/howlearningworks.

To read a QR code, you must have a smartphone or tablet with a camera. We recommend that you download a QR code reader app that is made specifically for your phone or tablet brand.

THE LEARNING PLAN WITH THE MODULES

This is a playbook and, by definition, contains a collection of tactics and methods used by a team to accomplish a common goal and get things done (Merriam-Webster, 2021d).

I.1 **GREAT LEARNING BY DESIGN**

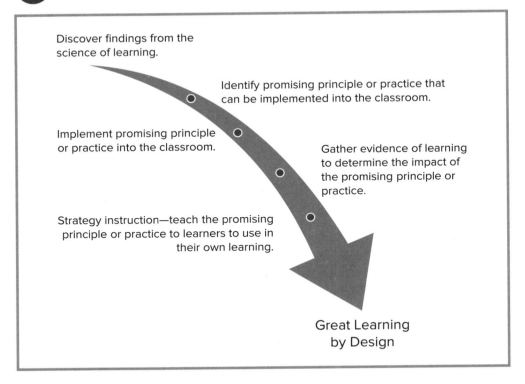

In the case of this playbook, the common goal is the translation of findings from the science of how we learn into promising principles or practices that can be implemented in classrooms and that students can utilize in their own learning journey. Therefore, each of the subsequent modules is designed to support your learning about this process. Just like the previous playbooks, the modules that follow this introduction are not necessarily intended to be completed in sequential order or all at once. When coaches and their teams go to their playbooks to get things done, they select the plays that best fit the current context or situation. For example, whether a football club (i.e., soccer team) uses an overlap, wall pass, spreads the ball wide, or has the winger whip in the cross depends on the current situation unfolding on the soccer field. The situation on a soccer field is fluid, as well as complex and multidimensional. Those last two descriptors should sound familiar—that is how we described the learning in Ms. Anderson's, Ms. Dixon's, and your classroom. The modules in this playbook should be utilized by your team when the current context or situation calls for the module. So, what's the plan?

This playbook is divided into four parts (see Figure I.2). The first part will unpack the science of learning by first developing a description of what is meant by learning in your classroom, the different ways of thinking about learning, barriers to learning, and discovering the major findings from the science of learning. What does it mean to learn something in your classroom? The science of learning offers promising principles or practices that *may* work in our classrooms. However, we must make *adaptations* to these principles or practices that reflect the *local context of the classroom* and then *generate evidence* that allows both us and our learners to determine if learning has occurred. Therefore, we must devote time to discover and develop a definition of what learning looks like in our individual classrooms, within the context of their content area

I.2 *HOW LEARNING WORKS* PLAYBOOK OVERVIEW

Section	Focus
Part I	
Module 1	What does learning look like in your classroom?
Module 2	What are different ways to think about learning?
Module 3	What are the barriers to learning?
Module 4	How do students learn?
Part II	
Modules 5–11	What are promising principles and practices?
Part III	
Modules 12–18	How do we translate promising principles and practices into learning strategies?
Part IV	
Module 19	How do we generate and gather evidence of impact?

and grade level. From there we will engage in a process for evaluating whether a specific finding from the science of learning is a promising principle or practice.

The second part of this playbook takes an up-close look at specific promising principles and practices from the science of learning. However, these modules will offer more than just an overview of the principle and examples. Instead, the emphasis in these modules will be on how to adapt the promising principles or practices/interventions based on the local context of individual classrooms (see Figure I.3).

I.3 IMPLEMENTING PROMISING PRINCIPLES AND PRACTICES

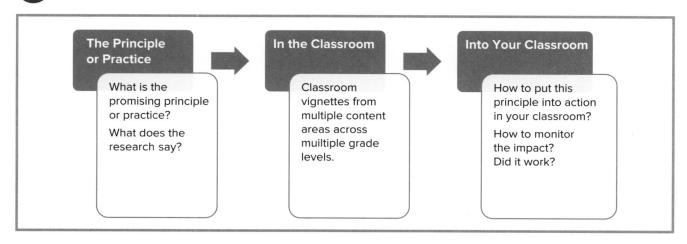

Then, we turn our attention to building the capacity in our students to take ownership of their own learning. Student learning strategies have the potential to considerably accelerate learning (Visible Learning Meta^X, 2021). This is the focus of Part III of this playbook. Summarizing, spaced practice, interleaved practice, elaborate interrogation, and transfer strategies are examples of tools that, when implemented effectively by students, move their learning forward.

Each module in this section will use the gradual release of responsibility to engage in strategy instruction with the learners in your classroom. As with the previous modules, there will be an emphasis on adapting the specific implementation of the learning strategy based on the local context of your individual classroom—using the learning strategies to overcome the barriers to learning (see Figure I.4).

online resources

For more resources related to learning strategies, visit the companion website at resources.corwin.com/howlearningworks.

I.4 LEARNING STRATEGY INSTRUCTION FROM PROMISING PRINCIPLES AND PRACTICES

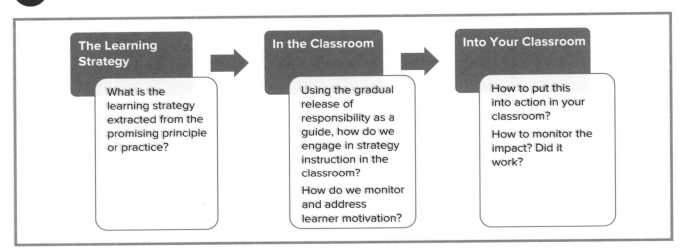

The Learning Strategy

What is the learning strategy extracted from the promising principle or practice?

In the Classroom

Using the gradual release of responsibility as a guide, how do we engage in strategy instruction in the classroom?

How do we monitor and address learner motivation?

Into Your Classroom

How to put this into action in your classroom?

How to monitor the impact? Did it work?

For a video on the significance of explicitly teaching students learning strategies, visit the companion website at resources.corwin.com/howlearningworks.

Learning strategy instruction will build the capacity and efficacy of students as they move beyond the specific learning experiences and outside of our classrooms. We want our students to take ownership of their learning and know what to do to move their learning forward when we are no longer their teacher. These modules support learners in

➡ Selecting the best learning tools to move their learning forward

➡ Seeking feedback about their learning

➡ Monitoring their own learning progress

➡ Making adjustments to their learning when necessary (Frey et al., 2018)

The final part of this playbook focuses on generating and gathering evidence of impact. Did the promising principles and practices result in student learning? The first aspect of evaluation is engaging in evaluative thinking and focusing on the need to generate evidence of learning. These final modules emphasize that we should see ourselves as evidence-generators that verify learning and challenge learners, not hold judgment over learning. The tasks within this module will lead to the development checks for understanding and provide opportunities for learners to respond, thus generating evidence of learning. This requires that we bring the learner directly into the conversation about their own learning. Using the evidence generated, how do we reframe the conversation away from grades (i.e., holding judgment over them and their learning) toward self-reflecting, self-monitoring, and self-evaluating their learning (e.g., one-on-one conferencing, error analysis, student-led conferences, goal setting, progress monitoring). The role of the teacher, then, is engaging in reciprocal and effective feedback that focuses on both the giving and receiving of information about learning.

For a video on the importance of evaluating the impact of this work, visit the companion website at resources.corwin .com/howlearningworks.

LEARNING WITHIN THE MODULES

Each of the modules has a specific focus, an explanation of the ideas within the module to establish purpose (a learning intention). The module then continues by linking the purpose of the module with specific findings from the science of learning. QR codes and the companion website provide resources that support the process of translating findings from the science of learning into classroom practice. In many instances, these are seminal works in the science of how we learn or the translation of the science into classroom practice. Don't be alarmed if you see a citation from the 1970s. That just means that particular study is either the first study to report a particular finding or is the "gold standard" for all subsequent work in this area. Examples of translation will cover primary, elementary, middle school, and high school content, skills, practices, dispositions, and understandings. From learning place value to writing an argumentative essay, we seek to provide a wide range of examples to show how the principles and practices potentially translate into our classrooms.

COLLABORATING FOR GREAT LEARNING

Each module offers you an opportunity for practice and application with a variety of grade levels and content areas. The practice section encourages you to write your answers and discuss them with your colleagues, if possible. Although using this book as part of your personal learning is possible, the translation and implementation of promising principles and practices are best done collectively with colleagues. We offer three suggestions for collaboratively using this playbook: an accountability partner, an instructional coach, or during your common planning or PLC+ meeting (see Fisher et al., 2020).

Let's start with accountability partners. The use of this playbook during common planning or your PLC+ meeting may not be feasible. You may be more comfortable partnering with a colleague across the hall, in another part of the building, or in another school.

You and this colleague can move through the modules, engage in the tasks, adapt the promising principles or practices/interventions based on the local context of each of your individual classrooms, and evaluate your impact. You and this colleague will serve as accountability partners in increasing your understanding of how learning works and leveraging your new learning in the design of your classrooms, learning experiences, and tasks.

A second way to collaboratively work with this playbook is alongside an instructional coach. Instructional coaches provide all of us with an outside perspective on the teaching and learning in our classrooms. They can provide us with the right feedback at the right time. Sitting down with an instructional coach, engaging in critical dialogue about how learning works, designing experiences and tasks, and then working together to evaluate the impact on student learning is an invaluable asset to our own professional growth.

Finally, this playbook can drive conversations during your PLC+ meeting (Fisher et al., 2020). We believe that the work of this playbook is another tool for the work you do in your PLC+. The use of these five guiding questions of PLC+ will keep the focus relentlessly on the learning of our students:

For a video on collaborating with the playbook, visit the companion website at resources.corwin.com/howlearningworks.

➡ Where are we going?

➡ Where are we now?

➡ How do we move learning forward?

➡ What did we learn today?

➡ Who benefited and who did not benefit? (Fisher et al., 2020, p. 8)

In PLC+, teachers identify learning intentions and discuss ideas for instruction. They meet to review student work and figure out if their efforts have been fruitful. They also talk about students who need additional instruction or support for success (Figure I.5). To revisit the earlier quote from Richard Mayer, "If you want to help people learn, it would be useful for you to know something about how learning works" (Mayer, 2011, p. vii). This is best done together, during our work as a community of learners.

Whether you have an accountability partner, access to an instructional coach, or a high-functioning, high-impact PLC+, the benefit of a collaborative approach is the opportunity to engage in critical dialogue around what learning looks like for you and your learners.

So, without any further delay, let's unpack how students learn!

I.5 HOW *HOW LEARNING WORKS* SUPPORTS THE WORK OF PLC+

PLC Question	*How Learning Works* Module
Where are we going?	Module 1. What Does Learning Look Like in Your Classroom? Module 2. What Are Different Ways to Think About Learning?
Where are we now?	Module 3. What Are the Barriers to Learning? Module 4. How Do Students Learn?
How do we move learning forward?	Module 5. Promising Principle 1: Motivation Module 6. Promising Principle 2: Attention Module 7. Promising Principle 3: Elaborate Encoding Module 8. Promising Principle 4: Retrieval and Practice Module 9. Promising Principle 5: Cognitive Load Module 10. Promising Principle 6: Productive Struggle Module 11. Promising Principle 7: Feedback
What did we learn today?	Module 12. Explicit Strategy Instruction Module 13. Learning Strategy 1: Goal Setting Module 14. Learning Strategy 2: Integrating Prior Knowledge Module 15. Learning Strategy 3: Summarizing Module 16. Learning Strategy 4: Mapping Module 17. Learning Strategy 5: Self-Testing Module 18. Learning Strategy 6: Elaborative Interrogation
Who benefited and who did not benefit?	Module 19. Generating and Gathering Evidence

PART I

In this section:

WHAT DOES LEARNING LOOK LIKE IN YOUR CLASSROOM?

LEARNING INTENTION

We are learning about the characteristics of learning in my classroom.

SUCCESS CRITERIA

I will know we have successfully completed this module when

- I can describe the different aspects of learning in my classroom.

- I can describe what learning is in my classroom.

The first sentence of this playbook used two very important words that need further exploring before we move forward in answering the essential question of this module. Write those two words below in the blanks provided.

not by __Chance__ *, but by* __design__

We enjoy etymology, the study of words. While that may not be a particularly enjoyable pastime for you, looking into the words *chance* and *design* can provide valuable insight and a sense of purpose for our work in this playbook. For example, the word *chance* has five different definitions in Merriam-Webster's Dictionary (2021a):

1. Something that happens unpredictably without discernible human intention or observable cause

2. A situation favoring some purpose (e.g., needed a chance to relax)

3. A fielding opportunity in baseball

4. The possibility of a particular outcome in an uncertain situation

5. Risk or a raffle ticket

Notice that each of these definitions is associated with a lack of control or predictability in the outcome. Even in the baseball example, the only example that seems not to fit into our conversation depends solely on whether the batter hits the ball in your direction. Hold on to these five definitions as we contrast them with the definitions of the word *design* (Merriam-Webster, 2021b).

1. To create, fashion, execute, or construct according to plan

2. To conceive and plan out in the mind, to have as a purpose, to devise for a specific function

3. *Archaic:* To indicate with a distinctive mark, sign, or name

4. To make a drawing, pattern, or sketch of, to draw the plans

For the word *design,* each of the four definitions implies a significant level of purpose, intentionality, and deliberation. This contrast in perspectives on learning cannot be overstated, especially when we are talking about the young learners in our schools and classrooms. Whether we are talking about equivalence in Ms. Anderson's first-grade classroom or transferable literacy skills in Ms. Dixon's English Language Arts block, the learning in both of these situations cannot be left to chance.

Using the space provided below, take a moment and reflect on the learning in your classroom. What aspect of your students' learning is left to chance? What aspects of your students' learning are by design? Yes, this task can be very challenging and put us in a vulnerable position. Do not feel compelled to share your thinking with your colleagues, but please take time to reflect on these questions. This reflection is an important part of our work in this playbook.

What Learning in Your Classroom Is Left to Chance?	What Learning in Your Classroom Occurs by Design?
my CR = the teachers a lot is left to chance	Staff meetings Staff Development Days Book Studies

online resources

For more resources related to learning by chance, visit the companion website at resources.corwin.com/howlearningworks.

Please mark the previous page, as we will return to this reflection as we move into subsequent modules.

Throughout the next several modules, we aim to move those examples of learning by chance and transition them to learning by design. The first step in this transition is to discover and develop a definition of what learning looks like in your classroom. This definition will serve as the plan, drawing, or sketch (Merriam-Webster, 2021b) necessary to design.

A DEFINITION OF LEARNING

If you surveyed 100 individuals and asked them what is meant by learning, you would likely get 100 different answers. However, those 100 answers are likely variations of beliefs about learning that could be organized into broader categories: behaviorism, cognitive learning theory, and constructivism (Schunk, 2019). For example, some believe that individuals learn through behavioral modification (see Figure 1.1).

1.1 SUMMARY OF THREE MAJOR LEARNING THEORIES

	Learning is . . .	The learner . . .
Behaviorism	. . . changing the probability that a specific behavioral outcome will occur by reinforcing or shaping behavior with a stimulus and response.	. . . is passive and the learning comes solely from the teacher as the source. In other words, they are an empty vessel that must be filled.
Cognitive	. . . knowledge stored in the cognitive architecture of the learner—memory—through processing, organizing, and synthesizing learning.	. . . is actively processing, organizing, and synthesizing learning, but the learning is considered independent of the learner.
Constructivism	. . . based on experiences and the construction of a personal interpretation of the world based on these experiences and interactions.	. . . is an active participant, constructing their own knowledge through collaboration, problem solving, and scaffolding.

Source: Adapted from Schunk (2019).

Those who approach learning from a **behavioral perspective** might describe learning as linking some stimulus, a specific type of mathematics problem, to a specific response, the algorithm for solving that problem. Likewise, a specific request to line up for lunch results in specific behaviors that have been reinforced over time.

If you take a **cognitive perspective**, you might respond that learning is the encoding and storing of information in memory. Through problem solving, deep processing, exploring, organizing, and synthesizing information, learners engage in active reading and use text features to make meaning of their reading. And if you are a **constructivist**, you might describe learning as the result of your students building their own personal interpretation of the world based on their experiences and interaction. In other words, learners construct their understanding of polygons in geometry, horizon lines and perspective in art, and spatial awareness in physical education through their active experiences.

Take a moment and develop your own definition of learning. What is meant by learning? Jot down your ideas and/or the ideas of your colleagues in the space below.

- connecting new material to what you already know
- social
- organizing information into usable chunks

If the previous task was challenging for you and your colleagues, you are not alone. You and your colleagues likely found it difficult to articulate learning as solely behavioral, cognitive, or constructive. Thinking through our school day, there are clear examples where stimulus-response learning was utilized and effective. We all have examples when cognitive processing was the focus and your students successfully organized and synthesized knowledge. Finally, you can think of times where your students were provided opportunities to construct personal meaning from these opportunities.

As teachers, devoting large amounts of time to unpacking and applying theories of learning is not only unhelpful but also does not reflect the complex and multidimensional nature of the learning in our classrooms. Learning is not behavioral, cognitive, or constructive. It's all three of these things, and more. Return to the introduction of this playbook and review the list you generated around the learning in Ms. Anderson's classroom. Learning is highly contextualized, meaning that the "where" of the learning and "who" is involved in that learning matters. Developing a universal view of learning is not going to result in great learning by design. Instead, we should develop a definition of what learning looks like in our own classrooms, for our learners. Using the template on the next page, gather evidence of how your own students feel about learning and themselves as a learner. This will be additional information that will allow us to see "who" is learning in our classroom and contextualize our definition of learning in the classroom. By the way, you can give this survey multiple times throughout the semester or year to see if your students change how they feel and what they think about learning.

online resources

For a Learning Survey Template, visit the companion website at resources.corwin.com/howlearningworks.

CONCEPTIONS OF LEARNING SURVEY

Directions: This survey is to gather information about how you see yourself as a learner and what you think about learning. Use the scales to mark what best represents your response to each statement.

I think . . .

1. Learning is when I am taught something I did not know before.	Strongly Agree — Agree — Disagree — Strongly Disagree
2. Learning is taking in as many facts as possible.	Strongly Agree — Agree — Disagree — Strongly Disagree
3. When someone gives me new information, I feel like I am learning.	Strongly Agree — Agree — Disagree — Strongly Disagree
4. Learning helps me understand and apply ideas.	Strongly Agree — Agree — Disagree — Strongly Disagree
5. Learning means I can talk about something in different ways.	Strongly Agree — Agree — Disagree — Strongly Disagree
6. When something stays in my head, I know I have really learned it.	Strongly Agree — Agree — Disagree — Strongly Disagree
7. If I have learned something, it means that I can remember that information whenever I want to or need it.	Strongly Agree — Agree — Disagree — Strongly Disagree
8. I should be able to remember what I have learned at a later date.	Strongly Agree — Agree — Disagree — Strongly Disagree
9. I have really learned something when I can remember it at a later date.	Strongly Agree — Agree — Disagree — Strongly Disagree
10. When I have learned something, I know how to use it in other situations.	Strongly Agree — Agree — Disagree — Strongly Disagree
11. If I know something well, I can use the information if the need arises.	Strongly Agree — Agree — Disagree — Strongly Disagree
12. Learning is making sense out of new information and ways of doing things.	Strongly Agree — Agree — Disagree — Strongly Disagree
13. I know I have learned something when I can explain it to someone else.	Strongly Agree — Agree — Disagree — Strongly Disagree
14. Learning is finding out what things really mean.	Strongly Agree — Agree — Disagree — Strongly Disagree
15. Learning is difficult but important.	Strongly Agree — Agree — Disagree — Strongly Disagree

(Continued)

(Continued)

16. Even when something I am learning is difficult, I must concentrate and keep trying.	Strongly Agree — Agree — Disagree — Strongly Disagree
17. Learning and studying must be done whether I like it or not.	Strongly Agree — Agree — Disagree — Strongly Disagree
18. Learning has helped me widen my views about life.	Strongly Agree — Agree — Disagree — Strongly Disagree
19. Learning changes my way of thinking.	Strongly Agree — Agree — Disagree — Strongly Disagree
20. By learning, I look at life in new ways.	Strongly Agree — Agree — Disagree — Strongly Disagree
21. Learning means I have found new ways to look at things.	Strongly Agree — Agree — Disagree — Strongly Disagree
22. Increased knowledge helps me become a better person.	Strongly Agree — Agree — Disagree — Strongly Disagree
23. I use learning to develop myself as a person.	Strongly Agree — Agree — Disagree — Strongly Disagree
24. When I learn, I think I can change as a person.	Strongly Agree — Agree — Disagree — Strongly Disagree
25. Learning is necessary to help me improve as a person.	Strongly Agree — Agree — Disagree — Strongly Disagree
26. I don't think I will ever stop learning.	Strongly Agree — Agree — Disagree — Strongly Disagree
27. I learn a lot from talking to other people.	Strongly Agree — Agree — Disagree — Strongly Disagree
28. Learning is gaining knowledge through daily experiences.	Strongly Agree — Agree — Disagree — Strongly Disagree
29. Learning is knowing how to get along with different kinds of people.	Strongly Agree — Agree — Disagree — Strongly Disagree
30. Learning is not only studying at school but also knowing how to be considerate of others.	Strongly Agree — Agree — Disagree — Strongly Disagree
31. Learning is the development of common sense in order to become a better member of society.	Strongly Agree — Agree — Disagree — Strongly Disagree
32. Learning is developing good relationships.	Strongly Agree — Agree — Disagree — Strongly Disagree

Source: Fisher et al. (2019).

So, let's try this again. Rather than developing an answer to the question *What is meant by learning?* develop a more contextualized description of learning in your classroom. Using the learning survey completed by your students as additional evidence, what does learning look like in your classroom? Be specific. If necessary, select an upcoming unit or topic and use that specific context to describe what learning looks like in your classroom.

As we wrap up our first module, our time devoted to discovering and developing a definition of what learning looks like in the context of our classrooms will help us better focus on the durable, flexible, and usable learning we strive for in our students. While there are many theories about learning, the contextualized nature of our classrooms requires that we devote time to articulating what learning is in Room 30, the gymnasium, the science laboratory, or the writing center. Then, and only then, can we create, fashion, and execute great learning according to plan—by design. In the next module, we will revisit your answer to the question *What is meant by learning?* and look at the different types of learning encompassed by your answer.

Oh, one last request. Using the blank pie chart on the next page, color in the percentage that reflects your belief about the responsibility for learning that falls to the teacher and the percentage of responsibility for learning that falls to the student. If possible, use two different colors. For example, you may believe that 90% of the responsibility falls to the teacher and 10% falls to the learner, so your chart might look like the following.

online resources

For more resources related to assessment-capable visible learners, visit the companion website at resources.corwin.com/howlearningworks.

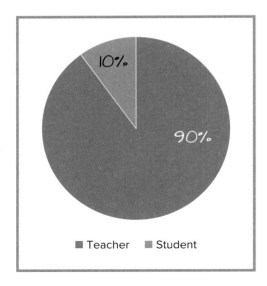

We will revisit this gauge several times over the remaining modules. For now, just color in and label your initial response below.

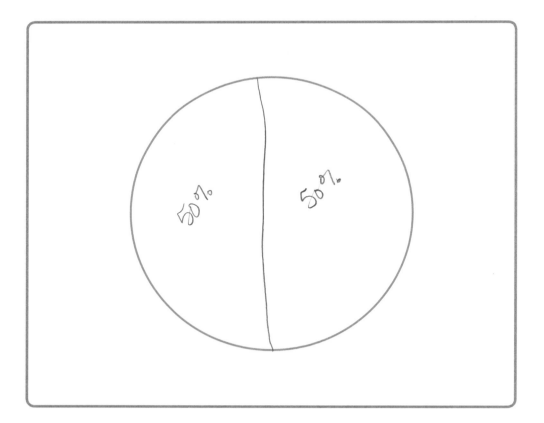

Checks for Understanding

Throughout the modules of this playbook, we want to provide multiple opportunities to model strategies that leverage the science of learning. One example of these strategies is a Know-Show Chart. The column on the left contains the success criteria from the beginning of this module except rephrased in the form of a question. The column on the right is for you to respond to those questions. Generate your responses to provide examples to support your responses that "show what you know."

Know	Show (Generate a response to the question that "shows what you know")
Can I describe the different aspects of learning in my classroom?	
Can I describe what learning is in my classroom?	

2

WHAT ARE DIFFERENT WAYS TO THINK ABOUT LEARNING?

LEARNING INTENTION

We are learning about specific components of the learning process.

SUCCESS CRITERIA

I will know we have successfully completed this module when

- I can compare and contrast the different components of learning in my classroom: declarative, procedural, and conditional knowledge.

- I can apply the process for learning to each component of that learning in my classroom.

Up to this point, we have devoted significant time to uncovering explicit and implicit learning in our classrooms (flip back to pages 1 and 2 in the introduction) and articulating what learning looks like in our individual classrooms (flip back to pages 13 and 15 in Module 1). We will spend one more module deconstructing what is meant by learning before diving into how students learn so that we can better design learning experiences that align with how learning works. To engage in the design of learning experiences that *translate* the science of how we learn into *promising principles and practices,* we must come to an understanding of learning in our local context—our own classroom with our learners. Returning to what learning looks like in your individual classroom (see pages 13 and 15), we need to look more closely at the different ways of thinking about that learning. Learning in our classrooms can be subdivided into **declarative, procedural**, and **conditional** knowledge. Before diving deeper into each of these subdivisions, let's start with an experiment.

How would you respond to the following question?

Do you know your multiplication facts? Circle your answer.

Yes   **No**

Odds are, you quickly circled *yes*, as you truly feel both comfortable and confident with your multiplication facts. Now consider this next question:

Why do you feel both comfortable and confident?

Our responses to the above question, and quite likely yours as well, communicate early experiences in our mathematics learning filled with timed drills or quizzes asking us to recall our 8's tables or 7's tables. We may even have a song for the 2's, 5's, and 10's. Now, try this next question:

What is 7×8? Show all of your thinking and work.

The previous series of questions bring to light the three different types of knowledge: declarative, procedural, and conditional. When looking specifically at 7 × 8, many of us likely paused and engaged in a series of internal strategies that lead us to the answer of 56. 56 was not an immediate answer and required some additional processing time. In fact, many of us likely hesitated in a way that we did not hesitate when originally asked "Do you know your multiplication facts?" For example, you may have started with 8 × 5 being equivalent to 40 and 8 × 2 being equivalent to 16. Then, adding them together equals 56. Others might have utilized tally marks to determine the final answer, while others used repeated addition to get to 56. Here's the point: while 7 × 8 first appears as a simple fact, there are other types of knowledge involved in this calculation—many that we overlooked with the initial question of simply knowing our multiplication facts.

THREE DIFFERENT TYPES OF KNOWLEDGE

Learning in our classrooms can be subdivided into declarative, procedural, and conditional knowledge.

LEARNING IN OUR CLASSROOMS CAN BE SUBDIVIDED INTO DECLARATIVE, PROCEDURAL, AND CONDITIONAL KNOWLEDGE.

Declarative knowledge is defined as the facts, figures, and details about a subject or content area. Declarative knowledge is the acquisition, consolidation, and storage of terminology, elements, theories, models, structures, or principles. In third-grade social studies, students learning that government exists at the community, state, and national levels must know the definitions of community, laws, and government. From there, they develop big ideas or principles that they can declare. For example, the purpose of laws is to keep people safe and maintain order.

Take a moment and return to the above example related to multiplication facts and 7 × 8. What aspects of the previous experiments are examples of declarative knowledge?

Procedural knowledge is all about knowing "how." In other words, procedural knowledge refers to the skills, processes, and algorithms associated with a subject or content area. Often represented as a series of steps, procedural knowledge requires learners to know when to apply specific skills, processes, and algorithms. Declarative and procedural knowledge are strongly linked together. For example, in solving systems of equations, learners must first know what systems of equations are and what their solutions represent or mean. That is declarative. Then, they must learn the different approaches, or procedures, for solving systems of equations (e.g., elimination, substitution, and graphing).

Take a moment and return to the above example related to multiplication facts and 7 × 8. What aspects of the previous experiment are examples of procedural knowledge?

And finally, **conditional knowledge** is knowing why and when to use declarative and procedural knowledge and when to pull from declarative knowledge and procedural knowledge to engage in new learning. Let's return to the previous example used in our defining of procedural knowledge. When acquiring, consolidating, and storing procedural knowledge about solving systems of equations, learners will begin to associate the procedures with specific characteristics of systems of equations (e.g., a constant in front of one variable and not the other or the same constant in both equations are equal). This association will help them build fluency in knowing when to use certain procedures for solving systems of equations and why one approach is more efficient than another.

Take one last look at the example related to multiplication facts and 7 × 8. What aspects of the previous experiment are examples of conditional knowledge?

The table below shows several examples of learning intentions. Using the space provided, identify the declarative, procedural, and conditional knowledge that may be associated with the learning intention in the first column. The first one is provided as an example.

For more resources related to meta-cognition, visit the companion website at resources.corwin.com/howlearningworks.

Learning Intention	Declarative Knowledge	Procedural Knowledge	Conditional Knowledge
Middle Grades Science: We are learning that the properties of an atom are based on the number and arrangement of subatomic particles.	What is an atom? What particles make up an atom? How are these particles arranged in an atom? How do subatomic particles interact?	How do I find the number of protons and electrons in an atom? How do I calculate the number of neutrons?	What is the relationship between valence electrons and how atoms participate in chemical bonding? What impact do the arrangement and number of subatomic particles have on the properties of an atom?
Personal Finance: We are learning about the features of a market economy.			
Elementary Language Arts (Reading): We are learning about the similarities and differences between two fictional texts.			

(Continued)

(Continued)

Learning Intention	Declarative Knowledge	Procedural Knowledge	Conditional Knowledge
High School Physical Education: We are learning how movement is created, directed, and stabilized in my lifetime fitness activities.			
Elementary Visual Arts: We are learning about the influence of culture on art.			
Elementary Character Education: We are learning about perseverance in meeting our goals.			
Elementary Language Arts (Writing): We are learning about narrative writing.			
High School World History: We are learning about the conditions that lead to Persia developing into the largest empire in the world.			

Before moving on, please return to your contextualized description of learning in your classroom from Module 1. Using different colors of pens, pencils, or highlighters, identify what in your description is declarative, procedural, or contextual. Also, now is the time to edit or revise your description. Now that you have had time to process Module 1, you may have details to add to your original description.

THREE PARTS OF THE LEARNING PROCESS

Developing declarative, procedural, and conditional knowledge does not occur in a single learning experience or through the completion of a single task. Again, learning is a process. While much attention has been given to describing this process (i.e., a blank slate, canvas, or computer), we find the best way to think about the learning process in our classrooms is to break the process down into three buckets (see Figure 2.1).

2.1   THREE PARTS OF THE LEARNING PROCESS

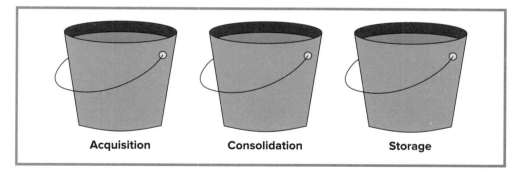

| Acquisition | Consolidation | Storage |

Source: Adapted from Mayer (2011). Image source: alijoy313/pixabay.com

Using the spaces below, come up with your own definition and description of each part of the learning process. When you can, provide specific examples from your classroom.

	Definition or Description	Examples From Your Classroom
Acquisition		
Consolidation		
Storage		

Keep this last task within reach. We will return to your definitions and descriptions several times over the next several modules to make edits and revisions. In addition, we will add more examples to the third column. For now, your responses will springboard us into the next module.

 ## Checks for Understanding

Take a moment and return to the success criteria for this module. As you did in the previous module, respond to the following questions by "showing what you know."

Know	Show (Generate a response to the question that "shows what you know")
Can I compare and contrast the different components of learning in my classroom: declarative, procedural, and conditional knowledge?	
Can I apply the process for learning to each component of that learning in my classroom?	

Now that we have a clear picture of what learning looks like in our classrooms, the different types (i.e., declarative, procedural, and conditional), and that learning is a process (i.e., acquisition, consolidation, and storage), we will now look at barriers to each part of the learning process. In Module 3 we will consider this question: What gets in the way of learning acquisition, consolidation, and storage?

3

WHAT ARE THE BARRIERS TO LEARNING?

LEARNING INTENTION

We are learning about challenges to the acquisition, consolidation, and storage of learning.

SUCCESS CRITERIA

I will know we have successfully completed this module when

- I can describe the different challenges to learning.

- I can recognize challenges to learning in my classroom using student data.

- I can hypothesize approaches to overcoming the challenges to learning in my classroom.

One way of thinking about the learning process is to break the process down into three main parts. Take a moment and write those three main parts, one on each of the buckets in Figure 3.1.

3.1 THREE PARTS OF THE LEARNING PROCESS

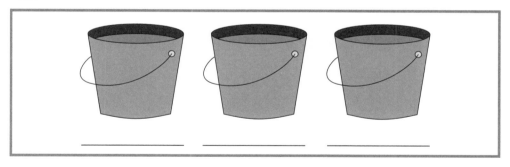

Source: Adapted from Mayer (2011). Image source: alijoy313/pixabay.com

ACQUISITION

When our students acquire new learning, they gain new content, skills, and understandings across all domains of learning. In science, this acquisition includes disciplinary core ideas, science and engineering practices, and crosscutting concepts (NGSS Lead States, 2013). In mathematics, this acquisition includes concepts, procedures, and the application of concepts and thinking (National Council of Teachers of Mathematics, 2014). In the visual arts, this includes acquiring critical thinking skills in the analysis, interpretation, and evaluation of the work of self and others (Virginia Department of Education, 2020). At the same time, learners acquire content, skills, and understandings related to language, social-emotional, and behavioral learning. For example, learners must acquire what it means to appropriately engage in a "morning meeting" and acquire the appropriate means for social interacting and relating to their peers.

There are several key points related to the acquisition part of the learning process that we want to emphasize:

➡ Learning acquisition is always happening, unconsciously or consciously. Flip back to page 13 in Module 1. Learning by chance is unconscious acquisition.

➡ In our classrooms, we strive for formalized learning through the design and implementation of learning experiences and tasks—not by chance, but by design. Again, returning to page 13 in Module 1, learning by design is conscious acquisition.

➡ There are many factors that influence acquisition, some internal and some external. We will address internal factors in this module and the external factors in subsequent modules.

➡ The acquisition of learning requires effective feedback. Learners must have the opportunity to engage in trial and error to acquire content, skills, and understandings.

Make a list of internal factors that influence acquisition. These are factors related to inner strengths or challenges in learners. Make a second list of external factors. These are factors within the learning environment and not the inner strengths or challenges in learners.

Internal Factors	External Factors

Take a moment and return to the closing task in the previous module. Edit and revise your definition, description, and examples of acquisition.

CONSOLIDATION

Learning takes time. After the initial acquisition of learning, our students need time to actively process this newly acquired content, skills, and understandings, as well as make meaning of their learning. For our classrooms, this involves us providing scaffolded learning experiences or tasks. These scaffolds should specifically align with the internal and external factors that influenced the initial acquisition of the learning. For example, if motivation was one of the internal factors you listed on the previous page, then consolidation should continue to scaffold or provide approaches to keep a learner motivated in the learning. How do we motivate learners to engage in science content, utilize mathematical processes, and apply critical thinking skills in the analysis of works of art?

Scaffolds are only scaffolds if they are withdrawn over time to promote self-regulated learning. Thus, with consolidation, these scaffolds should eventually be removed as learners internalize the content, skills, and understandings and are able to extend, apply, and transfer their learning.

Return to the previous lists of internal and external factors that influence learning acquisition. What role do these factors play in consolidating learning?

Take a moment and return to the closing task in the previous module. Edit and revise your definition, description, and examples of consolidation.

STORAGE

Effective acquisition and consolidation lead to learning storage. Often referred to as long-term storage, this is when the content, skills, and understandings are internalized and available for retrieval to then extend, apply, and transfer to other contexts. While initial acquisition and the subsequent consolidation are important, moving this learning to long-term storage is critical in extending, applying, and transferring learning. Now, to be clear, this does not mean that the content, skills, and understandings are permanently available for retrieval once storage occurs. Over time, there must be continued maintenance to support long-term storage. Think back to something that you acquired, consolidated, and stored. If enough time passes between the last retrieval of this learning from long-term storage, this learning may fade away.

Let's return to previous examples. Just because a learner has consolidated his or her learning about human impact on ecosystems does not immediately imply that he or she will, without intermittent retrieval and application of this consolidation. In mathematics, while solving systems of linear inequalities was at one time retrievable and available for transfer in solving, over time this learning is transient. If the critical thinking skills in the analysis, interpretation, and evaluation of the work of self and others are left alone for too long, these skills will need to be re-learned. And finally, appropriately engaging in social interactions, well, by the very nature of schools and life, is likely to stick around.

Return to the previous lists of internal and external factors that influence learning acquisition. What role do these factors play in long-term storage?

Take a moment and return to the closing task in the previous module. Edit and revise your definition, description, and examples of storage. Now, let's look at the factors influencing each of these parts of the learning process, in particular, the barriers to successful acquisition, consolidation, and storage.

CHALLENGES TO LEARNING BY DESIGN

In November 2020, Stephen Chew and his colleague William Cerbin compiled 20 years of research on teaching and learning by design, not by chance. Although they do not use the specific terminology of design and chance, they assert that the goal of pedagogical research is to amplify student learning through effective teaching. Yet, as we pointed out in the introduction of this playbook, learning is complex, multidimensional, and requires the careful design of learning experiences that result in both the learning of these ideas and the transfer of this learning to new contexts. To successfully design these learning experiences, we have to know who our learners are so that we can make the necessary adaptations based on the local context of our classrooms. This means that we must be aware of the specific challenges to learning by design. The result of Chew and Cerbin's compilation of research are nine specific challenges (see Figure 3.2).

online resources

For more resources related to cognitive challenges, visit the companion website at resources.corwin.com/howlearningworks.

3.2 OVERVIEW OF NINE SPECIFIC CHALLENGES TO LEARNING BY DESIGN

Challenge	Description
Student Mindframes	This refers to our learners' beliefs, attitudes, or dispositions about topics, content, or subject matter.
Meta-Cognitive Skills and Self-Regulation	This challenge refers to the capacity of our learners to self-monitor, self-reflect, and self-evaluate their knowledge, skills, and understandings.
Student Fear	How our learners feel about the classroom and content heavily influences their perception of learning experiences and tasks.
Insufficient Prior Knowledge	When our learners arrive in our classrooms with limited background knowledge, prior knowledge, and previous experiences, they may struggle in all three parts of learning.
Misconceptions	This challenge comes from learners having prior beliefs about specific topics, content, or subject matter that are inaccurate or incomplete.
Ineffective Learning Strategies	Challenges to learning can come from our learners relying on strategies that simply do not support the acquisition, consolidation, and storage of learning. These ineffective learning strategies create an illusion of learning.
Low Potential for Transfer	Learners may not have the capacity, yet, to transfer content, skills, and understandings.
Selective Attention Constraints	Challenges to learning may come from learners multitasking or not focusing on the relevant information or focusing only on part of the relevant information.
Working Memory Capacity	The challenge refers to the amount of mental effort available to learners and the limited capacity in their work memory. Too much information or information that is too complex will overwhelm learners.

Source: Adapted from Chew and Cerbin (2020).

There are three major points that we want to make sure are highlighted in our work in this playbook:

1. The nine challenges listed in Figure 3.2, in no particular order, can undermine the acquisition, consolidation, and storage of learning.

2. Our role in learning by design, not by chance, requires us to gather evidence about our learners with regard to these nine challenges. We must then use that evidence to create, fashion, and execute great learning according to plan—by design.

3. Student learning is not solely on the shoulders of the teacher, nor are these challenges so great that teaching and learning are not possible. Learners should aim to find the best way to learn from their teacher.

4. Using the blank pie chart below, color in the percentage that reflects your belief about the responsibility for learning that falls to the teacher and the percentage of responsibility for learning that falls to the student. If possible, use two different colors. For example, you may believe that 90% of the responsibility falls to the teacher and 10% falls to the learner.

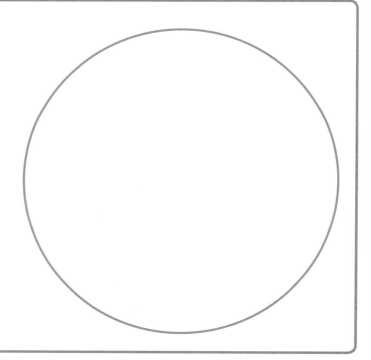

Let's revisit your pie chart from Module 1. In Module 1, you were asked to color in the percentage that reflects your belief about the responsibility for learning that falls to the teacher and the percentage of responsibility for learning that falls to the student. Has your belief changed as a result of your work in this playbook? If so, color in the percentages that reflect your current thinking. If not, simply replicate your response from Module 1.

As we close out this module, let's review where we are at this point in learning by design. Learning by design requires that we must make *adaptations* to principles or practices from the science of learning that reflect the *local context of the classroom* and then *generate evidence* that allows both us and our learners to determine if learning has occurred. These adaptations must reflect challenges to learning, those nine challenges uncovered by Chew and Cerbin (2020). The final task of this module is to think about and plan how you will generate and gather evidence from your learners about these challenges. How will you know which challenges you *and your students* must address as you strive to move learning forward in your classroom?

Use the space provided to plan how you will generate and gather evidence for each challenge. Some examples are provided to get your thinking started.

Challenge	Approaches for Generating and Gathering Evidence
Student Mindframes	**Develop an interest survey, discuss student responses during one-on-one conferences.**
Meta-Cognitive Skills and Self-Regulation	
Student Fear	
Insufficient Prior Knowledge	
Misconceptions	
Ineffective Learning Strategies	**Interview students about their "favorite" study strategy.**
Low Potential for Transfer	
Selective Attention Constraints	
Working Memory Capacity	**Student observation with various leveled problems or tasks.**

Checks for Understanding

Take a moment and return to the success criteria for this module. As you did in the previous modules, respond to the following questions by "showing what you know."

Know	Show (Generate a response to the question that "shows what you know")
Can I describe the different challenges to learning?	
Can I recognize challenges to learning in my classroom using student data?	
Can I hypothesize approaches to overcoming the challenges to learning in my classroom?	

Now, let's take what we have learned about learning and leverage that to move learning forward in our students.

4

HOW DO STUDENTS LEARN?

LEARNING INTENTION

We are learning about the promising principles and practices of learning.

SUCCESS CRITERIA

I will know we have successfully completed this module when

- I can self-evaluate my beliefs about how my students learn.

- I can explain the promising principles and practices of how my students learn.

- I can hypothesize approaches to overcoming the challenges to learning in my classroom.

Everyone has beliefs about how we learn and therefore how students learn. These beliefs come from our perceptions, interpretations, and how we make meaning of our past learning experiences. In addition, we are bombarded by images and statements from pop culture about learning. In many cases, these images and statements are attempting to convince us to download an app, take a supplement, or purchase an "instant fix" product to help our baby read or do math. What do you believe about how your students learn?

In the first few modules of this playbook, we described *what* learning looked like in our classrooms. Now, use the space provided and describe *how* students learn in your classroom with your students. At this point, we are transitioning from *what* to *how* in the playbook.

online resources

For more resources related to brain images, visit the companion website at resources.corwin.com/ howlearningworks.

In 2008, David McCabe and his colleague Alan Castel discovered the extent to which we hold on to our beliefs about learning and the influence of perceptions and interpretations on shaping those beliefs. Without a doubt or much disagreement, we can safely say that our brain is at the center of the learning process. Regardless of your particular orientation or theory about learning (see page 14 in Module 1), you can't talk about learning without referencing your brain. The brain is highly involved. However, this hyper focus on the brain can lead us to believe things about learning that may not actually be accurate. That is what McCabe and Castel (2008) found:

> Presenting brain images with articles summarizing cognitive neuroscience research resulted in higher ratings of scientific reasoning for arguments made in those articles, as compared to articles accompanied by bar graphs, a topographical map of brain activation, or no image. These data lend support to the notion that part of the fascination, and the credibility, of brain imaging research lies in the persuasive power of the actual brain images themselves. (p. 343)

And that is not even the best part of the research. The most shocking finding was that this phenomenon, an unchecked focus on the brain, worked for fictional neuroscience articles that were full of errors in the methodology, analysis, and conclusions of the article. That's right, junk articles with images of the brain were rated as more credible than articles that did not have images of the brain but instead had bar graphs or topographical maps. So, we have added images of brains to this playbook to enhance your perception of our credibility. Just kidding!

LEARNING MYTHS

Just as our students' misconceptions about learning pose challenges to their learning progress, our beliefs and misconceptions about how students learn can challenge our capacity to create, fashion, and execute great learning by design. Researchers have accumulated a list of beliefs and misconceptions about learning that are not supported by research and may actually interfere with our support of learning acquisition, consolidation, and long-term storage. Take a look at the following list of statements. First, simply read the statements to yourself. Then, go back and mark whether you think the statement is True or False.

1.	We use our brains 24 hours a day.	True	False
2.	It is best for children to learn their native language before a second language is learned.	True	False
3.	Boys have bigger brains than girls, on average.	True	False
4.	If students do not drink sufficient amounts of water, their brains shrink.	True	False
5.	When a brain region is damaged, other parts of the brain can take up its function.	True	False
6.	We only use 10% of our brain.	True	False
7.	The left and right hemispheres of the brain work together.	True	False
8.	Some of us are "left-brained" and some are "right-brained" and this helps explains differences in how we learn.	True	False
9.	The brains of boys and girls develop at different rates.	True	False
10.	Brain development has finished by the time children reach puberty.	True	False
11.	There are specific periods in childhood after which certain things can no longer be learned.	True	False
12.	Information is stored in the brain in networks of cells distributed throughout the brain.	True	False
13.	Learning is due to the addition of new cells to the brain.	True	False
14.	Individuals learn better when they receive information in their preferred learning style (e.g., auditory, visual, kinesthetic).	True	False
15.	Learning occurs through changes to the connections between brain cells.	True	False
16.	Academic achievement can be negatively impacted by skipping breakfast.	True	False
17.	A common sign of dyslexia is seeing letters backward.	True	False
18.	Normal development of the human brain involves the birth and death of brain cells.	True	False
19.	Mental capacity is genetic and cannot be changed by the environment or experience.	True	False
20.	Vigorous exercise can improve mental function.	True	False
21.	Children must be exposed to an enriched environment from birth to three years or they will lose learning capacities permanently.	True	False
22.	Children are less attentive after consuming sugary drinks and/or snacks.	True	False

(Continued)

(Continued)

23.	Circadian rhythms ("body-clock") shift during adolescence, causing students to be tired during the first lessons of the school day.	True	False
24.	Exercises that rehearse coordination of motor-perception skills can improve literacy skills.	True	False
25.	Extended rehearsal of some mental processes can change the structure and function of some parts of the brain.	True	False
26.	Children have learning styles that are dominated by particular senses (i.e., seeing, hearing, touch).	True	False
27.	Learning problems associated with developmental differences in brain function cannot be improved by education.	True	False
28.	Production of new connections in the brain can continue into old age.	True	False
29.	Short bouts of motor coordination exercises can improve integration of left and right hemisphere brain function.	True	False
30.	There are specific periods in childhood when it's easier to learn certain things.	True	False
31.	When we sleep, the brain shuts down.	True	False
32.	Listening to classical music increases children's reasoning ability.	True	False

Source: Dekker et al. (2012).

To check your answers, visit the companion website to access the article describing neuromyths and whether each of the above statements was True or False.

THE SCIENCE OF LEARNING

online resources

For more resources related to learning myths, visit the companion website at resources.corwin.com/howlearningworks.

As we check our own beliefs about learning, how do we get past the allure of brain images and our own misconceptions about learning? Having a clear understanding of how our students learn is both important and necessary if we are to amplify learning by design and not leave learning to chance. Plus, unless you have a CT scanner or fMRI machine in the back of your classroom, neuroscience research is not going to be much help in that design.

Over the past 100 years, cognitive scientists have accumulated a robust understanding of how we learn, including how students learn. This science of learning offers promising principles or practices that *may* work in our classrooms.

Take a moment and use an electronic device to look up "the science of learning." Using the space provided, summarize the definition of the science of learning.

And as we have said in the introduction to this playbook, we must make *ad_____s* to these principles or practices that reflect the *lo__l c_____t of the classroom* and then *generate ev_____e* that allows both us and our learners to determine if learning has occurred. Those promising principles or practices relate to the following significant areas from the science of learning:

1. Motivation

2. Attention

3. Elaborate Encoding

4. Retrieval and Practice

5. Cognitive Load

6. Productive Struggle

7. Feedback

⟩⟩⟩ Checks for Understanding

Take a moment and return to the success criteria for this module. As you have done in the previous modules, respond to the following questions by "showing what you know."

Know	Show (Generate a response to the question that "shows what you know")
Can I self-evaluate my beliefs about how my students learn?	
Can I explain the promising principles and practices of how my students learn?	
Can I hypothesize approaches to overcoming the challenges to learning in my classroom?	

Now, let's start with motivation.

PART II

In this section:

5

PROMISING PRINCIPLE 1: MOTIVATION

As we move into our first promising principle or practice derived from the science of learning, we want to recall how we plan on tackling each of these ideas and translating them to our own classrooms (see Figure 5.1).

5.1 **A FRAMEWORK FOR TRANSLATING THE SCIENCE OF LEARNING AND MOTIVATION INTO A PROMISING PRINCIPLE OR PRACTICE**

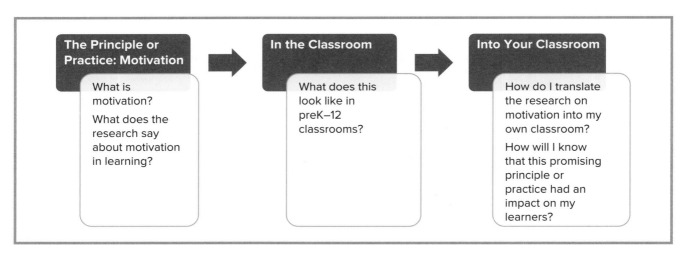

The Principle or Practice: Motivation

What is motivation?

What does the research say about motivation in learning?

In the Classroom

What does this look like in preK–12 classrooms?

Into Your Classroom

How do I translate the research on motivation into my own classroom?

How will I know that this promising principle or practice had an impact on my learners?

In this module, along with Modules 6–11, we will take an overview of the research on motivation and the science of learning. From there, we will look at specific examples of how classrooms have translated this research into promising principles and practices with a close look at how classrooms have monitored the impact of these principles and practices on student learning. Then, we will develop ways to translate research on motivation into the local context of our own, individual classrooms.

LEARNING INTENTION

We are learning about the role of motivation in my students' investment in learning.

SUCCESS CRITERIA

I will know we have successfully completed this module when

- I can describe what is meant by motivation.

- I can explain the different ways of thinking about motivation in my classroom.

- I can develop specific ways to apply research on motivation into my classroom and evaluate the impact of this application.

WHAT IS MOTIVATION?

Motivation is an overarching term that refers to the reason or reasons associated with a particular action. In classrooms, this refers to the general desire of learners to engage in the learning experiences or tasks. This may also reflect the willingness of learners to uphold the expectations for being a member of the classroom learning community (e.g., norms and processes for social interactions, moving from one area of the classroom or building to another). Motivation is an essential component of the science of how we learn simply because the learning expected in our classrooms will only move forward if learners have the desire or willingness to commit the necessary effort to acquire, consolidate, and store declarative, procedural, and conditional knowledge.

What motivates your learners? Use the space provided to develop a list or description of what motivates your students in your classroom.

So, when it comes to motivating students to engage in learning about equivalence, over-hand throwing, figurative language, right triangle trigonometry, or soil chemistry, there are four components that manifest as the reasons, desires, and willingness to exert the effort necessary for learning. These four components are *personal, activated, energized,* and *directed* (see Figure 5.2).

5.2 THE FOUR COMPONENTS OF MOTIVATION

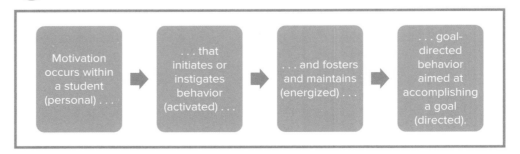

Source: Adapted from Mayer (2011).

The research on motivation brings forward several findings that will help us translate research from the science of learning into a promising principle or practice:

1. **Interest/Attitude (Effect Size = 0.46).** Learners show increased motivation in putting forth effort in the acquisition, consolidation, and storage of learning when that learning is of interest to them and toward which they have a positive attitude (Visible Learning Meta[X], 2021).

2. **Self-Efficacy (Effect Size = 0.66).** Learners are motivated by the belief that their efforts in learning will pay off or provide some immediate or long-term benefit to them (Visible Learning Meta[X], 2021).

3. **Effort-Based Attributions/Student Expectations (Effect Size = 0.77).** If learners are able to link their efforts in learning to specific outcomes, both positive and negative, they are more likely to put forth effort in succeeding in their learning (Visible Learning Meta[X], 2021).

4. **Deep Motivation (Effect Size = 0.57).** Deep motivation occurs when our learners want to develop competency, mastery, and deeper understanding to have a fuller understanding of overall content, skills, and understandings (Visible Learning Meta[X], 2021).

5. **Cooperative Learning (Effect Size = 0.46).** A pedagogical strategy through which two or more learners collaborate to achieve a common goal. Typically, cooperative learning programs seek to foster positive interdependence through face-to-face interactions, hold individual group members accountable for the collective project, and develop interpersonal skills among learners (Visible Learning Meta[X], 2021).

6. **Prior Achievement/Success (Effect Size = 0.59).** As learners have mastery experiences or experience success in a specific area, their motivation to further engage and persist in future learning experiences or tasks goes up. Prior achievement and success help builds learners' efficacy, raise expectations, and improve their overall attitude and dispositions toward learning (Visible Learning Meta[X], 2021).

online resources

For more resources related to motivation, visit the companion website at resources.corwin.com/howlearningworks.

Return to the list or description of what motivates the students in your classroom. Organize that list based on the findings on the facing page. Which ones are examples of interest/attitude? Self-efficacy? Expectations or deep motivation? What about cooperative learning? Use the space to organize your thinking.

WHAT DOES THIS PRINCIPLE OR PRACTICE LOOK LIKE IN THE CLASSROOM?

Before we dive into specific examples, we want to take a moment and talk about the motivation for extracting promising principles or practices from the science of learning. Promising principles and practices are often sought because of a recognized problem of practice. Consider the following problems of practice identified by teachers we have the pleasure of interacting with on a regular basis:

PROMISING PRINCIPLES AND PRACTICES ARE OFTEN SOUGHT BECAUSE OF A RECOGNIZED PROBLEM OF PRACTICE.

➡ "My learners never remember the basic formulas for find the area and perimeter of irregular polygons."

➡ "My students always forget to cite evidence from the text when responding to text-based questions."

➡ "When students are involved in physical activity, I am always reminding them of how to operate in a safe space."

➡ "They never study. I can barely even get them to ask questions before the test."

➡ "My students don't seem to want to talk. When I ask them to engage in a think-pair-share, they so often sit in silence and wait for time to pass."

➡ "My high schoolers won't read. I can ask them to read a novel, but they find every way possible to avoid having to read it."

➡ "My learners view themselves as 'bad at art.' This way of thinking interferes with their willingness to devote time and effort to their art projects. They rush through tasks and attribute their poor performance to their belief that they are 'bad at art.'"

Each of the above examples indicates a particular challenge or problem in the classroom that would motivate you and me to actively seek to solve. Thus, we will dig into the science of learning and look for possible findings that can be translated into practice and improved learning outcomes.

Take a moment and return to the examples of problems of practice. Circle, highlight, or underline the problems of practice that you believe are linked to motivation. The hard part is that many of these could be linked to motivation, while also being linked to other challenges (e.g., fear, misconceptions, prior knowledge, selective attention, or working memory). That is the beauty of this playbook: in addition to unpacking these promising principles and practices, we will devote time to developing ways of measuring our impact. In other words, was the challenge or problem of practice really about motivation, or something else? If it was something else, we will have to dig further and try other promising practices. But for now, let's look at some examples of how research on motivation and the science of learning can be extracted and applied to the problems of practice listed above (see Figure 5.3).

5.3 EXTRACTING PROMISING PRINCIPLES AND PRACTICES FROM MOTIVATION RESEARCH TO THE CLASSROOM

Problem of Practice	Potential Promising Principle or Practice	Ways to Evaluate the Impact	Link to the Research on the Science of Learning
"My learners never remember the basic formulas for find the area and perimeter of irregular polygons."	Rather than pure memorization, the teacher taught learners how to derive the formulas so that they had a deep understanding of not just what the formulas were, but why they were what they were.	Student work samples before and after the intervention; did the learners provide more details in their work or explanations of their work?	Deep Motivation
"My students always forget to cite evidence from the text when responding to text-based questions."	To motivate learners to commit more effort to this particular aspect of the learning, the teacher implements "proofreading pals" that provide feedback on their responses to text-based questions.	In-class tasks and exit tickets; did learners cite evidence in their independent tasks more frequently after working with their "proofreading pals"?	Cooperative Learning With Peers

Problem of Practice	Potential Promising Principle or Practice	Ways to Evaluate the Impact	Link to the Research on the Science of Learning
"When students are involved in physical activity, I am always reminding them of how to operate in a safe space."	The teacher provided hula-hoops for her and her learners to stand in during instruction. Together, both the teacher and learners worked on developing a sense of their safe space.	Classroom observation and the number of reminder slips during physical education block; did learners increase their self-monitoring of their safe space?	Cooperative Learning With the Teacher
"They never study. I can barely even get them to ask questions before the test."	The teacher provided video recordings of previous students describing their study habits and how they helped them succeed in their learning. Then, the teacher explicitly taught those strategies to the learners.	Student survey asking about their study habits before and after the intervention and student performance on assessments; did learners report using more effective study habits? Did the use of the study habits correlate with their performance on the assessment?	Effort-Based Attributions and Student Expectations
"My students don't seem to want to talk. When I ask them to engage in a think-pair-share, they so often sit in silence and wait for time to pass."	This classroom teacher developed a series of tasks that tapped into students' interests as a practice for motivating them to engage in classroom discussion.	Classroom observation; using a checklist, did learners engage in more dialogue, using academic vocabulary?	Interest/Attitude
"My high schoolers won't read. I can ask them to read a novel, but they find every way possible to avoid having to read it."	The English Department implemented goal setting and reading logs to encourage students to divide up their reading into smaller, more manageable chunks.	Progress monitoring of the reading logs; was there a change in the time devoted to reading? Did the nature of classroom discussions about the reading change?	Self-Efficacy
"My learners view themselves as 'bad at art.' This way of thinking interferes with their willingness to devote time and effort to their art projects. They rush through tasks and attribute their poor performance to their belief that they are 'bad at art.'"	This classroom teacher decides to explicitly teach specific techniques and elements of art, providing opportunities to develop these techniques. This also helps learners experience success and recognize that they can be successful.	Use student work before and after the explicit instruction of techniques; ask learners to describe their process and how the process leads to the specific piece of artwork. Do learners begin to approach their artwork as a process and not simply a task to complete? What language do they use to talk about their artwork and themselves as an artist?	Prior Achievement/Success

Looking at the examples in the first column of Figure 5.3, there is a possibility, as we noted, that the challenge is not related to motivation, but to some other aspect of acquiring, consolidating, and storing learning. How will you know if the principle or practice related to motivation worked? Well, as you can see in the third column, we must generate and gather evidence that will help us answer the question. This is known as evaluative thinking and is a key component of successfully implementing what works best in learning.

Evaluative Thinking About Learning

1. What is the learner ready to learn, and what evidence supports this?

2. What are possible interventions from the science of learning?

3. What is the expected impact and how will this be measured?

4. How will the possible intervention from the science of learning be implemented in my classroom with my learners (i.e., adaptations based on the local context)?

5. Did the intervention have an impact?

6. How do I collaborate with colleagues and peers to interpret the evidence of impact?

Source: Adapted from Rickards et al. (2021).

We have captured and rephrased questions 2–5 of evaluative thinking in a template for you to use in your own classroom and with your colleagues and learners. Why the change in questions? Well, we wanted to provide guiding questions for you and your accountability partner, instructional coach, or PLC+. These questions direct our focus on applying promising principles with intention and purpose—moving learning forward through a challenge or problem of practice. Let's give it a try.

HOW DO WE IMPLEMENT THIS PRINCIPLE AND PRACTICE INTO OUR CLASSROOMS?

Use the next pages to map out your own challenge of problem of practice. You can return to Figure 5.3, column 4, for examples of an aspect of the learning in your classroom that you might want to focus on.

Challenge or Problem of Practice:

What evidence do you have that this is a challenge or problem of practice with your learners (e.g., observations, conversations, entrance tickets, exit tickets, attendance data, assignment submission)?

Describe the promising principle or practice you want to use.

Link the promising principle or practice to research from the science of learning on motivation. Refer back to the previous information in this module if necessary.

Describe, in as much detail as possible, how you will implement this promising principle or practice. Again, refer back to Figure 5.3 for examples.

How will you collaborate with your accountability partner, instructional coach, or PLC+ team to determine if your promising principle or practice worked? What evidence would convince you and your colleagues that the principle or practice did not work?

Motivation is an aspect of learning that will need continuous monitoring and adjusting. What is an impetus for effort on Monday may not be as effective on Wednesday. What moves learners to devote resources to learning in the morning may not do the same later in the day. If we are to have great learning by design, a reflective process will need to become a regular part of learning.

⟩⟩⟩ Checks for Understanding

Take a moment and return to the success criteria for this module. As you have done in the previous modules, respond to the following questions by "showing what you know."

Know	Show (Generate a response to the question that "shows what you know")
Can I describe what is meant by motivation?	
Can I explain the different ways of thinking about motivation in my classroom?	
Can I develop specific ways to apply research on motivation into my classroom and evaluate the impact of this application?	

However, we cannot simply stop at motivation. Once we have created a general desire of learners to engage in the learning experiences or tasks, we must move our attention to what they are paying attention to in the experience or task—the topic of the next module.

6

PROMISING PRINCIPLE 2: ATTENTION

Learners may be motivated to put effort into the acquisition, consolidation, and storage of declarative, procedural, and conditional learning, but if they do not direct their attention to the right aspects of the learning task or experience, they will likely not meet the learning expectations (see Figure 6.1).

6.1 A FRAMEWORK FOR TRANSLATING THE SCIENCE OF LEARNING AND ATTENTION INTO A PROMISING PRINCIPLE OR PRACTICE

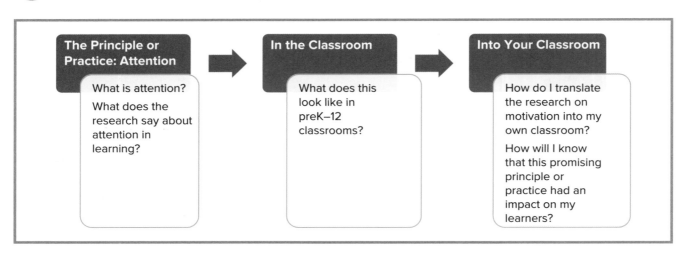

The Principle or Practice: Attention

What is attention?

What does the research say about attention in learning?

In the Classroom

What does this look like in preK–12 classrooms?

Into Your Classroom

How do I translate the research on motivation into my own classroom?

How will I know that this promising principle or practice had an impact on my learners?

LEARNING INTENTION

We are learning about the role of attention in my students' learning.

SUCCESS CRITERIA

I will know we have successfully completed this module when

- I can describe what is meant by attention.

- I can explain the influences on my students' attention to learning in my classroom.

- I can develop specific ways to apply research on attention into my classroom and evaluate the impact of this application.

WHAT IS ATTENTION?

To acquire, consolidate, and store content, skills, and understandings in the classroom, learners must attend to that particular learning. Let's look at a specific example by starting with the explicitly stated learning intentions and success criteria for a middle grades social studies class in North Carolina.

TODAY'S LEARNING INTENTIONS

Content Learning Intention: We are learning about the scarcity of resources in settlements.

Language Learning Intention: We are learning about the role of historical narratives in communicating events and experiences.

Social Learning Intention: We are learning about the value of diverse perspectives in communicating about historical events and experiences.

SUCCESS CRITERIA

We will know we are successful when

- We can identify the physical features of a specific geographic location that *might* influence the settlement.

- We can provide evidence of how those physical characteristics influenced the settlement.

- We can cite evidence from historical narratives to support our inferences.

This is the declarative, procedural, and conditional learning that is expected in this classroom on a given day. If this is the expected learning, then this particular teacher must design learning experiences and tasks that direct learners' attention to the most relevant content, skills, and understandings. Furthermore, these experiences and tasks must also support learners in discerning what is irrelevant to their progress toward the learning intentions and success criteria.

ATTENTION IS OUR CAPACITY FOR IDENTIFYING, SELECTING, AND FOCUSING OUR COGNITIVE RESOURCES ON SPECIFIC STIMULI.

For a video on attention and awareness, visit the companion website at resources.corwin.com/howlearningworks.

Attention is our capacity for identifying, selecting, and focusing our cognitive resources on specific stimuli. When we are successful at this endeavor, or when we leverage this capacity, we are successful at discerning between what is relevant and irrelevant and then holding that attention until a specific goal or outcome is accomplished. In the classroom, this goal or outcome is the successful acquisition, consolidation, and storage of learning. Selective attention, or directing our attention to relevant stimuli, is powerful in ensuring that learners focus on the right content, skills, and understandings at the right moment, and for the amount of time necessary for great learning by design.

Take a moment and participate in a brief experiment. Using the QR code provided, take a look at the brief video and instructions associated with one of the most famous selective attention experiments from the science of learning and attention.

So, how did the experiment go? According to Simons and Chabris (1999), if individuals have never heard of "the invisible gorilla," about 50% of participants never notice his entrance or exit in the video clip.

But what if you have heard of "the invisible gorilla" before ever reading this playbook? Does this influence your selective attention? Well, Chabris and Simons took that into consideration and designed a subsequent experiment to see what prior knowledge of the gorilla did to participants' attention. For additional information about this second experiment, visit the companion website.

As interesting as this experiment and conversation are, let's turn our attention back to the importance of this particular finding from the science of learning and our classrooms. Use the Venn diagram below to compare "the invisible gorilla" experiments to your classroom. Be very specific. Include the details of Simons and Chabris' experiment to really unpack the value in including the current discussion in this playbook.

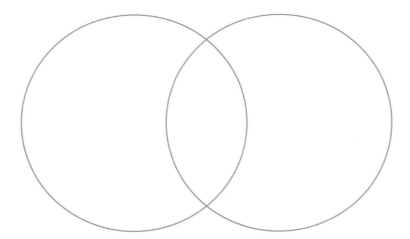

online resources

For more resources related to the original Simons and Chabris study, visit the companion website at resources.corwin.com/howlearningworks.

Let's return to the seventh-grade social studies classroom. Just as the teacher provided learning intentions and success criteria for the learners, Simons and Chabris (1999) provided a goal for us in the video. The subsequent tasks in the social studies class must align to those learning intentions and success criteria just as the individuals passed the basketball in the experiment. But, if counting the number of passes between participants is really what we are looking for as the goal or outcome, what factors must we consider?

These factors are already familiar to us in classrooms. Take a moment, use the space provided, and list specific influences that you believe affect your learners' attention.

FACTORS INFLUENCING ATTENTION

There are several factors influencing our attention and the attention of our learners. The effect sizes for each factor are from the Visible Learning Meta^X (2021) database.

1. **Prior Knowledge and Learning (Effect Size = 0.93).** What our learners already know, understand, and are able to do influences where we direct our attention. Unless purposefully, intentionally, or deliberately directed elsewhere, our learners will attend to elements of a learning experience or task that is familiar to them or that they already know, understand, and are able to do.

   Return to the learning intentions and success criteria from the seventh-grade social studies class. How might attention to the relevant aspects of the learning be supported through *prior knowledge and learning*? Use the space provided to brainstorm ideas.

For another video on attention and awareness, visit the companion website at resources.corwin.com/howlearningworks.

> LEARNERS NEED SCAFFOLDING AND SUPPORT AS THEY DEVELOP THEIR OWN CAPACITY IN DISCERNING RELEVANT AND IRRELEVANT ASPECTS OF THEIR LEARNING.

2. **Deep Motivation (Effect Size = 0.57).** Yes, the promising principle or practice from Module 5 is related to the promising principle or practice in this module. Simply put, when our learners are motivated to learn something, they are more likely to pay attention. However, that still does not mean they will pay attention to the most relevant aspects of the learning experience or task. This is where our responsibility really plays out in the design of the learning. We have to design learning to ensure that this motivation to learn is directed toward the most relevant aspects of the experience or task, but then scaffold our learners' capacity to self-regulate their own attention. This is the focus of the second half of this playbook.

   Use the space provided to describe the relationship between motivation and attention. Revisit Module 5 if a quick review is necessary.

3. **Awareness/Attention/Engagement (Effect Size = 0.54).** The smell of a science experiment, an image of a battle in World War II, the suspense in a short story, or the anticipation of playing a game tap into our body's emotional system. This, in turn, diverts our attention to the source of these emotional stimuli.

Brainstorm ideas about ways to "capture" your learners' attention. List them in the box below, alongside the specific learning goals or outcomes.

WHAT DOES THIS PRINCIPLE OR PRACTICE LOOK LIKE IN THE CLASSROOM?

Capturing and maintaining the attention of learners toward relevant aspects of the learning experience or task is something that must be continuously monitored and adjusted throughout each and every day. In addition, learners need scaffolding and support as they develop their own capacity in discerning relevant and irrelevant aspects of their learning. While having clear learning intentions and success criteria is a start, some other promising principles and practices can be extracted and implemented in our classroom. As we indicated in Module 5, the power of this implementation comes from our evaluating the impact of each promising principle or practice on learning. Let's look at some examples of how research on attention and the science of learning was extracted and applied to these specific situations (see Figure 6.2).

online resources

For more resources related to dual coding theory and cognitive load, visit the companion website at resources.corwin.com/howlearningworks.

6.2 EXTRACTING PROMISING PRINCIPLES AND PRACTICES FROM ATTENTION RESEARCH TO THE CLASSROOM

Challenge or Problem of Practice	Potential Promising Principle or Practice	Ways to Evaluate the Impact	Link to the Research on the Science of Learning
"I have a very difficult time getting my learners to pay attention to the language of *Hamlet* and notice key details in the written word of a play. They are used to watching a play."	Rather than simply introducing *Hamlet* as simply reading a Shakespearean drama, a high school English teacher introduces *Hamlet* describing the plot in modern terms (e.g., you come home from college and find your mother married to your uncle; oh, and he is haunted by his father's ghost).	Learners were asked to identify five scenes and explain how that scene is critical in the development and resolution of the play; learners focused on the specific elements and language, ignoring those aspects that were not pertinent to the outcome.	Emotional Cueing
"Students don't always see the value in studying ancient civilizations. They just brush it off as studying dead people."	Rather than opening up the lesson or the first lesson of the unit with the traditional presentation of the learning intentions and success criteria, the teacher provided specific examples of "things from today" that are from those ancient civilizations (e.g., aqueducts in Rome and plumbing; Greco-Roman ideas of citizenship and assemblies paired with the U.S. Constitution).	Through independent tasks, did learners identify additional connections and provide explicit links to course topics? They did not get distracted by other aspects of the civilizations.	Providing Meaning and Relevancy
"When my students arrive in the gymnasium, it is chaos. They don't always pay attention to instructions given for the day's lesson. They get distracted by the equipment and ignore me when I explain the agenda for the day."	The teacher decided to break down the process for entering the gymnasium into specific steps, presented one by one to the learners. In addition, the teacher provided specific time spans for learners to complete that particular step—using a timer for guiding learners.	The teacher monitored the amount of time at the beginning of class devoted to behavior and management; the efficiency and effectiveness of learners getting ready to learn; their knowledge and awareness of the learning expectations for the class (i.e., did they recognize the most relevant aspects of the introduction?).	Avoid Multitasking
"I find it very difficult for my learners to make it through the block. I can barely work through two examples before they checkout."	Recognizing that learners cannot pay continuous attention for the entire mathematics block, the teacher breaks the block into 7- to 10-minute chunks, offering learners opportunities to refocus on other tasks between those chunks (e.g., think-pair-share, turn and talk, or taking a break completely).	Are learners asking and responding to questions at a great frequency during the 7- to 10-minute chunks? Are learners engaging in my self-reflection and self-monitoring during the think-pair-shares or turn and talks?	Allow for Breaks

HOW DO WE IMPLEMENT THIS PRINCIPLE AND PRACTICE INTO OUR CLASSROOMS?

Use the space below to map out your challenge or problem of practice. You can return to Figure 6.2 for examples of an aspect of your students' attentiveness to learning in your classroom that you might want to focus on in this module.

Challenge or Problem of Practice:

What evidence do you have that this is a challenge or problem of practice with your learners (e.g., observations, conversations, entrance tickets, exit tickets, attendance data, assignment submission)?

Describe the promising principle or practice you want to use.

Link the promising principle or practice to research from the science of learning on attention. Refer back to the previous information in this module, if necessary.

Describe, in as much detail as possible, how you will implement this promising principle or practice. Again, refer back to Figure 6.2 for examples.

How will you collaborate with your accountability partner, instructional coach, or PLC+ team to determine if your promising principle or practice worked? What evidence would convince you and your colleagues that the principle or practice did not work?

Are the questions in the above boxes embedded in your approach for extracting and implementing a promising principle or practice from the science of learning on attention? Remember, if our learners are not paying attention, the acquisition, consolidation, and storage of learning will be almost impossible during your designed learning experience or task.

⟩⟩⟩ Checks for Understanding

Take a moment and return to the success criteria for this module. As you have done in the previous modules, respond to the following questions by "showing what you know."

Know	Show (Generate a response to the question that "shows what you know")
Can I describe what is meant by attention?	
Can I explain the influences on my students' attention to learning in my classroom?	
Can I develop specific ways to apply research on attention into my classroom and evaluate the impact of this application?	

Motivation, attention—now let's take a look at encoding.

7

PROMISING PRINCIPLE 3: ELABORATE ENCODING

John Medina (2014) asserts that "the more elaborately we encode information at the moment of learning, the stronger the storage" (p. 110). But what does this mean? Well, just as we invoked "the invisible gorilla" experiment in the previous module, let's try another experiment here. For this experiment, adapted from the one provided in John Medina's book, *Brain Rules*, you will need the help of your colleagues or your PLC+.

1. Divide them into two groups.

2. One group should count and tally the number of letters that contain diagonal lines and the number of letters that do not have diagonal lines.

3. The other group should determine if the word gives them a positive or negative feeling and why.

4. Then, show them the list of words below and allow them to look at the list for two minutes.

Nine	Cell	Ring
Sword	Apple	Table
Army	Fire	Worm
Clock	Color	Baby
Desk	Rock	Bird

5. Once the two minutes have expired, hide the list of words and ask your colleagues to write down as many words as they can recall from the list.

6. Tally up the number of words for each group.

The surprising and shocking results bring us to the focus of this module. The second group of your colleagues engaged in elaborate encoding, the third promising principle of this playbook (see Figure 7.1). Before moving forward, look back at the details of this experiment and reflect on the similarities and differences in the specific task for each group. Use the space provided and the guiding questions to jot down your thoughts.

How were the tasks of the two groups in the previous experiment similar? How were they different?

Based on your observations from this experiment, summarize what is meant by elaborate encoding.

7.1 A FRAMEWORK FOR TRANSLATING THE SCIENCE OF LEARNING AND ELABORATE ENCODING INTO A PROMISING PRINCIPLE OR PRACTICE

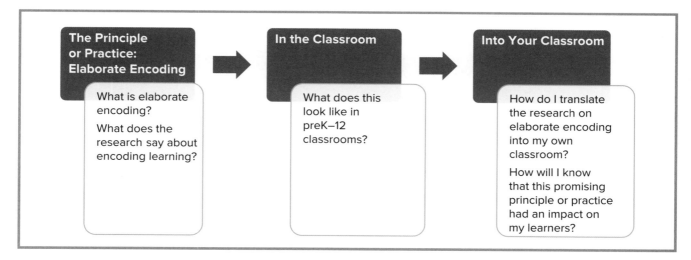

The Principle or Practice: Elaborate Encoding

What is elaborate encoding?

What does the research say about encoding learning?

In the Classroom

What does this look like in preK–12 classrooms?

Into Your Classroom

How do I translate the research on elaborate encoding into my own classroom?

How will I know that this promising principle or practice had an impact on my learners?

LEARNING INTENTION

We are learning about elaborate encoding and how it amplifies student learning.

SUCCESS CRITERIA

I will know we have successfully completed this module when

- I can describe what is meant by elaborate encoding.

- I can compare and contrast elaborate and rote encoding in learning.

- I can develop specific ways to apply research on elaborate encoding into my classroom and evaluate the impact of this application.

WHAT IS ELABORATE ENCODING?

Returning to the word list at the beginning of this module, the second group was asked to engage in a deep level of processing by focusing on their emotional reactions and then explaining that reaction. This is very different from counting letters with diagonal lines. Elaborate encoding is the deep processing of information by linking new content, skills, and understandings to prior knowledge, background knowledge, and/or previous experiences. One way to think about elaborate encoding is through Wittrock's generative processes (see Doctorow et al., 1978). Let's try this process using a piece of text.

Locate a newspaper or magazine article or any piece of text you have access to in your home, classroom, or office. As you read the text, pause at the end of each paragraph and write a summary of that paragraph in your own words. This generative process, the

For more resources related to elaborate encoding, visit the companion website at resources.corwin.com/ howlearningworks.

active engaging in the text by first reading and then summarizing the reading, promotes elaborate encoding and leads to better learning.

This seminal work paved the way for subsequent research in the science of learning related to elaborate encoding. When learners engage in elaborate encoding, they engage in deeply processing the learning. This leads to better acquisition, consolidation, and storage of learning.

online resources

For more resources related to generative processes, visit the companion website at resources.corwin.com/howlearningworks.

online resources

For more resources related to elaboration and thought to action, visit the companion website at resources.corwin.com/howlearningworks.

COMPONENTS OF ELABORATE ENCODING

There are three contributors to elaborate encoding that support this deeper processing. **First and foremost, motivation.** Yes, this is becoming a reoccurring theme. Learners must be motivated to devote their time, attention, and effort to the elaborate encoding experience or task. If this motivation is absent in our classrooms, learners may default to the equivalent of counting letters with diagonal lines (e.g., summarizing their notes versus memorizing vocabulary terms).

Second, elaborate encoding requires multiple representations of the content, skills, and understandings. When we refer to multiple representations, we are referring to mental representations or different ways of thinking about the learning. Summarizing content in their own words, self-questioning, creating or associating the learning with visuals and imagery, and constructing graphic organizers with the material are examples of multiple representations.

Finally, elaborate encoding encourages learners to find and apply patterns within their learning. This is different from simple repeating patterns. Consider the following example from an elementary mathematics classroom.

Option 1	Option 2
Directions: Complete the following.	**Directions:** Complete the following.
$6 + 10 = ?$ $7 + 9 = ?$ $8 + 8 = ?$ $9 + 7 = ?$ $10 + 6 = ?$	1. Choose any number between 2 and 9. 2. Add that number to itself, write the equation, and solve. 3. Then, increase the number you picked by one and decrease the number you picked by one. 4. Add those two new numbers. 5. Repeat this process a few more times. What do you notice?

Source: Adapted from Hattie et al. (2017).

How are Options 1 and 2 similar? How are they different?

Which of these options requires learners to find and apply patterns? Which one simply requires the repeating of patterns? In this case, Option 2 is an example of elaborate encoding and will promote greater acquisition, consolidation, and storage. Now, there is a very valuable place in the learning process for Option 1, but we will address this in the next module.

Use the space provided and brainstorm different ways to incorporate elaborate encoding into the learning in your classroom.

> LEARNERS MUST BE MOTIVATED TO DEVOTE THEIR TIME, ATTENTION, AND EFFORT TO THE ELABORATE ENCODING EXPERIENCE.

	Potential Ways to Incorporate Into the Learning in My Classroom
Motivation	
Multiple Representations	
Finding and Applying Patterns	

APPROACHES TO PROMOTING ELABORATE ENCODING

While there are many approaches to supporting elaborate encoding in learning, there are some very common approaches that we will focus on as examples of deriving promising principles or practices from this aspect of the science of learning.

➔ Summarizing Learning Into Learners' Own Words (Effect Size = 0.74). One approach to foster multiple representations and the finding and applying of patterns is to ask learners to summarize content, skills, and understandings into their own words. This can be done in writing or through verbal communication. In the science classroom, learners can turn and talk to peers, for example, to summarize the Krebs Cycle in cellular respiration.

➔ Self-Questioning (Effect Size = 0.59). As learners engage in declarative, procedural, and conditional learning, students can generate their own questions and then develop answers to those questions. These should be questions that require them to clarify their understanding, probe their conceptual understanding, and inquire into their procedural knowledge. For example, after reading the assigned pages in *Silas Marner*, learners can generate questions about their reading and then answer their own questions.

➔ Visuals and Imagery (Effect Size = 0.51). The platitude that a picture is worth 1,000 words is good advice for elaborate encoding. Linking words and numbers to images provides multiple representations and allows for pattern identification. For example, in a mathematics class, learners would benefit from seeing the equation to a particular function, along with the table for that function and the corresponding graph. Of course, they could summarize the elements of that equation and generate questions about the equation that they would then answer.

➔ Concept Mapping (Effect Size = 0.64). Finally, deep levels of processing are supported through concept mapping. However, in this case, concept mapping is more than just circles connected by lines. The goal here would be to generate statements or sentences that explain why two particular circles are connected.

> **THE PLATITUDE THAT A PICTURE IS WORTH 1,000 WORDS IS GOOD ADVICE FOR ELABORATE ENCODING.**

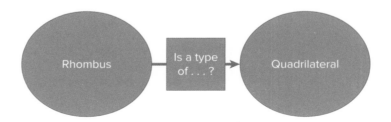

Let's look at each of these in the context of the classroom and how to evaluate the impact of the promising principles or practices on student learning (see Figure 7.2).

WHAT DOES THIS PRINCIPLE OR PRACTICE LOOK LIKE IN THE CLASSROOM?

 7.2 EXTRACTING PROMISING PRINCIPLES AND PRACTICES FROM ELABORATE ENCODING RESEARCH TO THE CLASSROOM

Challenge or Problem of Practice	Potential Promising Principle or Practice	Ways to Evaluate the Impact	Link to the Research on the Science of Learning
"My students simply memorized chemical formulas and did not understand the why behind the Krebs Cycle in cellular respiration. This is more than just chemical formulas."	The teacher asks learners to summarize the Krebs Cycle in their own words with a partner and then on their own in an exit ticket. Their summaries were to include specific examples.	The teacher monitors the use of scientific terminology and the ability for learners to talk about the Krebs Cycle in relation to other cellular processes. Did learners respond to transfer-type questions on the end-of-unit assessment?	Summarizing
"My learners just read words. They don't take on the role of an active reader and seek to comprehend the text. To them, the book is simply words on a page and not a quality piece of literature."	As learners read the novel *Silas Marner*, they had to generate different types of questions and respond to them. These questions were kept in their reading notebooks and used for individual, partner, and group tasks during the unit.	Were learners able to make inferences and cite specific evidence from the text in written assignments and during class discussions? Were learners able to reference specific aspects of the plot and relate those details to the development of the characters?	Self-Questioning
"My learners do not fully understand that variables and constraints on equations are real things and not some abstract idea. This is the essence of mathematical modeling."	The teacher decides to use equations, tables, and graphs together in learning about linear equations. This teacher uses technology to ensure that learners can make changes to an equation and immediately see those changes in the table and graph (e.g., Desmos).	Classroom observations of learners' discussions and questions; student work samples before and after the intervention; did the learners provide more details in their work or explanations of their work?	Visuals and Imagery
"The learners struggle to see relationships between vertices, sides, and geometric shapes. They try to just memorize characteristics."	The teacher decides to use graphic organizers that require learners to organize information, identify relationships, and apply those relationships to additional geometric shapes.	Classroom observation; using a checklist, did learners use relationships in new learning? Was there a shared language in discussing shapes? How did learners perform on unit assessments that include different types of geometric shapes?	Concept Mapping
"My learners do not always learn the essential characteristics of different periods in art history. To them, they 'all look the same.'"	The art teacher decides to have learners create a series of thinking maps that compare and contrast different periods that are very similar on the surface.	Classroom observation; student conversations when analyzing different pieces of art; essays—use to explain the essential characteristics for each period.	Concept Mapping

As you review the specific examples in this table, keep in mind that we will devote several modules to building our learner capacity to self-regulate their own learning. For now, simply use these examples to develop your own hypotheses about how this promising principle can be extracted and implemented in your classroom to support learning.

HOW DO WE IMPLEMENT THIS PRINCIPLE AND PRACTICE INTO OUR CLASSROOMS?

Use the next pages to map out your challenge or problem of practice. You can return to Figure 7.2 for examples of elaborate encoding in your classroom that you might want to focus on in this module.

Challenge or Problem of Practice:

What evidence do you have that this is a challenge or problem of practice with your learners (e.g., observations, conversations, entrance tickets, exit tickets, attendance data, assignment submission)?

Describe the promising principle or practice you want to use.

Link the promising principle or practice to research from the science of learning on encoding. Refer back to the previous information in this module, if necessary.

Describe, in as much detail as possible, how you will implement this promising principle or practice. Again, refer back to Figure 7.2 for examples.

How will you collaborate with your accountability partner, instructional coach, or PLC+ team to determine if your promising principle or practice worked? What evidence would convince you and your colleagues that the principle or practice did not work?

))) Checks for Understanding

Take a moment and return to the success criteria for this module. As you have done in the previous modules, respond to the following questions by "showing what you know."

Know	Show (Generate a response to the question that "shows what you know")
Can I describe what is meant by elaborate encoding?	
Can I compare and contrast elaborate and rote encoding in learning?	
Can I develop specific ways to apply research on elaborate encoding into my classroom and evaluate the impact of this application?	

After encoding, we now turn our attention to retrieval and practice.

8

PROMISING PRINCIPLE 4: RETRIEVAL AND PRACTICE

In our previous module, we considered the promising principle and practice of elaborate encoding. Take a moment and, in your own words, jot down everything you can remember from the previous module. Do not look back at the previous module—do this using purely recall.

Now, flip back to Module 7 and fill in any missing details or correct any inaccurate information about elaborate encoding. How much did you recall about elaborate encoding? What did you leave out and have to go and retrieve from the previous module? This task, while very similar to an ordinary review of previous materials, sets us up for a look at retrieval and practice. However, before we go any farther into this module, let's try one more task.

Take a look at the seven images of what appear to be pennies. You will quickly notice that they are all different. Your task in this experiment is to try to identify the one image that accurately depicts a penny. Please do not go and find a penny to help you. Try to identify which image looks like a penny.

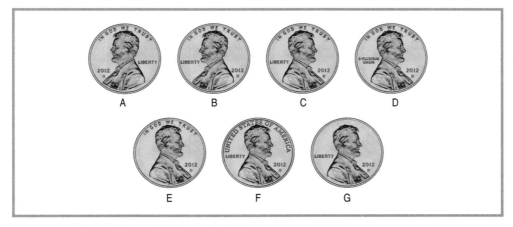

Image source: Editorial Image, LLC/Alamy Stock Photo

online resources

For more resources related to long-term memory for a common object, visit the companion website at resources.corwin.com/howlearningworks.

Before we reveal the answer, let's think about the two previous tasks. We just completed Module 7, but likely had to return to the content of that module to fill in missing information in the review box. Additionally, we have seen, touched, and used thousands of pennies in our lifetime. Yet, we likely could not identify an image that accurately depicts a penny. Why is that?

If we devoted the time, attention, and effort to Module 7, there is a high likelihood that we elaborately encoded the information about elaborate encoding. This elaborate encoding comes from the experiences and tasks embedded in that module. For the penny task, we may have seen, touched, and used thousands of pennies, but there is a high likelihood that we did not pay attention to or elaborately encode the details or features of what pennies look like while using them. (By the way, the answer is C.) You did not elaborately encode those details or features because you did not need them—no motivation. Yet, we struggled with both tasks. Simply put, the initial encoding of declarative, procedural, and conditional knowledge is not enough. We have to retrieve and practice learning to ensure long-term acquisition, consolidation, and storage of that learning (see Figure 8.1).

8.1 A FRAMEWORK FOR TRANSLATING THE SCIENCE OF RETRIEVAL AND PRACTICE INTO A PROMISING PRINCIPLE OR PRACTICE

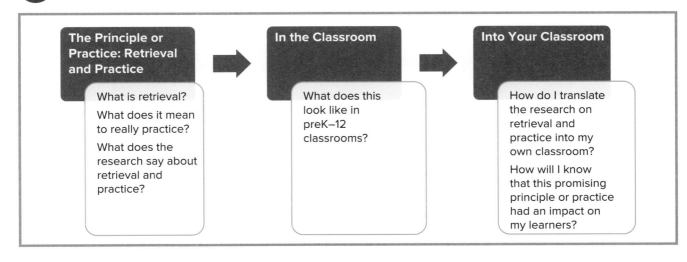

The Principle or Practice: Retrieval and Practice

What is retrieval?

What does it mean to really practice?

What does the research say about retrieval and practice?

In the Classroom

What does this look like in preK–12 classrooms?

Into Your Classroom

How do I translate the research on retrieval and practice into my own classroom?

How will I know that this promising principle or practice had an impact on my learners?

WHAT IS RETRIEVAL AND PRACTICE?

Retrieval is the act of "going and getting" declarative, procedural, and conditional knowledge. Once learning is acquired, encoded, and stored, the act of retrieval is the reactivation of that learning through active processing. For example, consolidation and long-term learning call for retrieving the characteristics of quadrilaterals, the process for finding the genotype and phenotype, the importance of author purpose in a piece of writing, or the conditions for starting cardio-pulmonary resuscitation (CPR). The act of "going and getting" information is well-documented in the research as a means of increasing the consolidation and storage of learning (Bjork, 1975; Roediger & Karpicke, 2006). In the box below are several statements from the research on retrieval. However, rather than simply providing these research findings to you in a bulleted list, let's utilize the process of retrieval. Complete the following fill-in notes about retrieval.

1. Instead of repeated restu_____g, learners are far better off tes_____g themselves, both early and often.

2. This does not mean that we admin_____r more tests, but rather provide numerous opp_____s for students to retr_____e previously learned information from memory.

3. The act of retr_____l is a memory modi_____r. Whatever infor_____n is retr_____d becomes strengthened.

4. With fee_____k, either by seeing the answers or rev_____g the information, the benefits of tes_____g become even more powerful.

5. For mult____e-ch____e questions, have students justify why a particular answer is cor____t and why other answers are incor____t.

6. When material is studied over sev____l sess____s and tested in a new context, var____g the contexts of study results in be____r perf____ce.

The answers:

1. restudying; testing

2. administer; opportunities; retrieve

3. retrieval; modifier; information; retrieved

4. feedback; reviewing/revising/revisiting; testing

5. multiple-choice; correct; incorrect

6. several sessions; varying; better performance

Before moving forward, take a moment and brainstorm the possible implications on your classroom of these findings from the science of learning about retrieval. How might these three specific findings from the science of learning translate into your classroom?

online resources

For more resources related to retrieval, visit the companion website at resources.corwin.com/ howlearningworks.

Research Finding About Retrieval	Possible Application to My Classroom
Learners are far better off testing themselves, both early and often.	
Provide learners with numerous opportunities to retrieve previously learned information from memory.	
Mistakes are okay! When learners make mistakes, receive feedback, and have the opportunity to revise the information, the benefits of retrieval are enhanced.	
Varying the context of retrieval enhances the benefit as well.	

We will return to the implementation of retrieval into our classrooms soon. For now, we want to tackle two important aspects of retrieval: timing and type. First, what about the timing of retrieval?

TIMING OF RETRIEVAL

When should we retrieve and how much time between each retrieval is optimal in boosting learning? To answer these two questions, consider the following graph of data. Take some time and look closely at the graph.

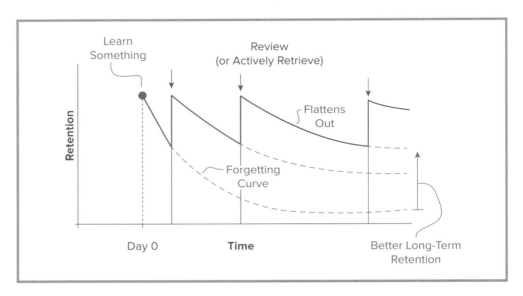

When you are ready, use the space provided to write down your observations about this graph. What do you notice? What stands out to you? How does this graph help us see the relationship between retrieval and time?

Retrieval should be approached much like drinking the recommended daily allowance of water. We should drink smaller amounts of water throughout the entire day, not consume the recommended daily allowance all in one dose first thing in the morning or right before we go to bed. Furthermore, we should take these smaller drinks of water right before we become thirsty. Likewise, we should space out retrieval during the learning experience, day, week, or unit AND offer opportunities to retrieve just as learners are about to forget. With this new learning, return to the space on the previous page and add any additional observations that stand out in the graph. Also, take a moment and revisit the table of findings from the science of learning on retrieval. With this additional learning about the spacing of retrieval, what additional applications are you now thinking about for your own classroom?

TYPES OF RETRIEVAL PRACTICE

We have talked about the power of retrieval and the nature of the timing for that retrieval. Before closing out this module, let's talk about the type of retrieval by looking at two different ways to practice. There are two different types of retrieval practice: naïve practice and deliberate practice (Ericsson & Pool, 2016). **Naïve practice** is practice that simply accumulates experience. This type of practice is typically without purpose and represents simply going through the motions (Ericsson et al., 1993).

In mathematics, an example of naïve practice would be learners playing mathematics games simply because that was the next task in their rotation or on the agenda. Another example would be learners simply calculating the area of a triangle over and over again because that was the assignment.

For science, naïve practice would be learners repeatedly going over the parts of a flower, reviewing the steps of the rock cycle, or calculating the density of various substances. Another example of naïve practice is writing a word 10 times, or 100 times for that matter, thinking that it improves spelling. Similarly, memorizing dates and facts using flashcards is not likely to ensure deep understanding of ancient civilizations or the geography of a specific region. While this supports memorization, the flexibility and adaptability of this type of knowledge are limited (i.e., limited transfer).

In **deliberate practice,** learners pinpoint a particular piece of content, a practice, or a disposition on which they want to improve. Then, learners focus their time on specifically improving in that particular content, practice, or disposition until it can be integrated into other learning. Deliberate practice is a mindful and structured way of learning by targeting areas needing improvement (Ericsson et al., 1993).

In mathematics, a learner may recognize that they struggle with adding fractions with unlike denominators. Deliberate practice could still involve having the learner play a game, but the game should be chosen intentionally to target this area of need and should focus on strategies to find a common denominator and then add the fractions. If a learner found multistep contextualized problems confusing, deliberate practice would involve acting out, sketching, or visualizing and talking out similar problems to make sense of them but not worry about actually solving them yet; thus, the learning focuses on the targeted area of need in a structured way.

In science, a learner may recognize that she has considerable difficulty in balancing equations, especially in oxidation-reduction reactions. For spelling, deliberate practice

DELIBERATE PRACTICE IS A MINDFUL AND STRUCTURED WAY OF LEARNING BY TARGETING AREAS NEEDING IMPROVEMENT.

online resources

For more resources related to deliberate practice, visit the companion website at resources.corwin.com/howlearningworks.

might involve repeated spelling "tests" in which the learner analyzes the location in the word where the error occurred and then focuses his learning on that spelling pattern, generalizing to other words with a similar pattern (to note, we recognize that not all words in the English language work this way).

Deliberate practice focuses on a particular piece of content, a specific skill, or a partial understanding as learners strive to improve their knowledge in that area. If a learner encountered problems understanding the relationship between human actions and the environment, he or she would engage in deliberate, spaced practice sessions that targeted this concept and his or her understanding of the concept. If a learner encountered challenges remembering the differences between ancient Greece and ancient Rome, deliberate and spaced practice sessions would need to help him or her improve their learning in these areas.

With practice, learners deepen their consolidation and storage of their learning. The step from initial acquisition to the long-term storage of declarative, procedural, and conditional knowledge is accomplished through deliberate practice.

Yet, we cannot stop there. As evidenced by the forgetting and remember curves on page 80, learners need to engage in maintenance. This requires learners to continue to retrieve to maintain their learning. Now, let's implement retrieval and practice into our classrooms (see Figure 8.2).

WHAT DOES THIS PRINCIPLE OR PRACTICE LOOK LIKE IN THE CLASSROOM?

8.2 EXTRACTING PROMISING PRINCIPLES AND PRACTICES FROM RETRIEVAL AND PRACTICE RESEARCH TO THE CLASSROOM

Focus	Ways to Deliberately Practice	How Will Learners and Teachers Know They Need to Deliberately Practice?	Opportunities for Naïve Practice
Areas of polygons using the composition of familiar polygons	Use manipulatives, sketches, folding, and visualizing to compose and decompose polygons. Have students find in their environment or create mystery shapes and find their areas.	Hold conferences to identify areas of struggle in problem solving. Discuss explanations and reflections within problem-solving tasks. Share and discuss feedback on formative assessments, such as exit tasks and hinge questions.	Sketch quick images of composed and decomposed polygons. Find areas of mystery shapes as weekly may-do tasks.

Focus	Ways to Deliberately Practice	How Will Learners and Teachers Know They Need to Deliberately Practice?	Opportunities for Naïve Practice
The law of conservation of mass in isolated systems	Offer different homework assignments based on areas needing improvement; use small group instruction; use a learning contract.	Provide feedback to learners on entrance and exit tickets. Support students in answering their own questions.	Continue to put questions relating to this topic on upcoming entrance tickets, exit tickets, and other assessments.
Sight words	Read vocabulary-controlled and decodable texts.	During small group reading instruction, help learners recognize which words they have mastered and which require additional instruction and/or practice.	Use a flashcard app to practice words. Read words from the word wall chorally as a class. Send lists of sight words home with parents to practice.
The influence of China and Korea on ancient Japan	Read from a variety of sources on the subject based on areas of need. Watch videos on the learning management system (LMS) that provide needed information based on the practice test.	Use a formative practice test to identify areas of strength and need. Ask students to analyze their results and develop study plans.	Create a graphic organizer or note page. Take the quizzes in the LMS that provide corrective feedback and opportunities to re-take them.

Source: Adapted from Almarode et al. (2021).

Again, we will devote several modules to building our learners' capacity to self-regulate their own retrieval and practice. After all, managing deliberate practice for 30 different learners at different locations in their learning progression is not sustainable. For now, simply use these examples to develop your own hypotheses about how this promising principle can be extracted and implemented in your classroom to support learning.

HOW DO WE IMPLEMENT THIS PRINCIPLE AND PRACTICE INTO OUR CLASSROOMS?

Retrieval and practice are more than "drill and kill." Retrieval and practice are intentional, purposeful, and deliberate actions by the learner that seek to close gaps in the learning. These gaps are not to be interpreted as a deficit in the learner, but simply the pathway for moving learners from where they are to where they are going (e.g., expectations, learning intentions, and success criteria). To avoid us falling into the trap of naïve practice, or practice for the sake of practice, take a moment and review the big ideas in this module. Use the t-chart below to list characteristics and examples of these two approaches to retrieval and practice.

Deliberate Retrieval and Practice	Naïve Retrieval and Practice

Use the next pages to map out your challenge or problem of practice. You can return to Figure 8.2 for examples of elaborate encoding in your classroom that you might want to focus on in this module.

Challenge or Problem of Practice:

What evidence do you have that this is a challenge or problem of practice with your learners (e.g., observations, conversations, entrance tickets, exit tickets, attendance data, assignment submission)?

Describe the promising principle or practice you want to use.

Link the promising principle or practice to research from the science of learning on encoding. Refer back to the previous information in this module, if necessary.

Describe, in as much detail as possible, how you will implement this promising principle or practice. Again, refer back to Figure 8.2 for examples.

How will you collaborate with your accountability partner, instructional coach, or PLC+ team to determine if your promising principle or practice worked? What evidence would convince you and your colleagues that the principle or practice did not work?

⟫⟫ Checks for Understanding

Take a moment and return to the success criteria for this module. As you have done in the previous modules, respond to the following questions by "showing what you know."

Know	Show (Generate a response to the question that "shows what you know")
Can I identify the benefits of retrieval and practice on my students' learning?	
Can I describe the conditions of retrieval and practice that improve student learning?	
Can I develop specific ways to apply research on retrieval and practice into my classroom and evaluate the impact of this application?	

After retrieval and practice, we now turn our attention to cognitive load.

9

PROMISING PRINCIPLE 5: COGNITIVE LOAD

Below is a picture of an object, familiar to many of us, a surge protector. This particular object will play a role in the unpacking of our current promising principle, cognitive load. Using the space provided, describe the purpose and benefits of using a surge protector. This particular ask has a point and sets us up for what is coming next.

Image source: iStock/rjp85

OUR COGNITIVE ARCHITECTURE PROVIDES SIMILAR PROTECTION AGAINST INFORMATION OVERLOAD.

In your above response, you likely referenced purposes and benefits such as plugging in multiple devices, the availability of USB plug-ins, and, just maybe, you mentioned that the surge protector protects your devices from sudden bursts of energy (e.g., lightning). Just as a surge protector prevents a sudden burst of energy from damaging your electronic devices, our cognitive architecture provides similar protection against information overload. To be clear, this comparison breaks down in that learning is not quite equivalent to electricity and if learners take on too much information, they will not experience damage to their cognitive architecture. They will, however, forget much of the learning when this happens just as a surge protector stops devices from working when overloaded with electricity. This is the basis for understanding cognitive load theory. Knowing what is meant by cognitive load and taking steps to ensure that we do not inadvertently trigger our learners' built-in "surge protectors" by exceeding our learners' cognitive load will support our learners as they encode, consolidate, and store the essential declarative, procedural, and conditional learning we strive for in our classrooms. This leads us to the promising principles and practices of cognitive load (see Figure 9.1).

For more resources related to cognitive load theory, visit the companion website at resources.corwin.com/ howlearningworks.

9.1 A FRAMEWORK FOR TRANSLATING THE SCIENCE OF LEARNING ON COGNITIVE LOAD INTO A PROMISING PRINCIPLE OR PRACTICE

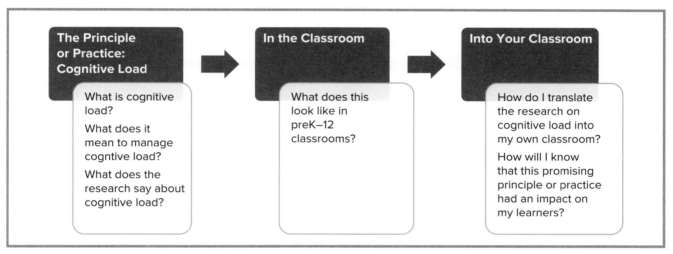

The Principle or Practice: Cognitive Load

What is cognitive load?

What does it mean to manage cogntive load?

What does the research say about cognitive load?

In the Classroom

What does this look like in preK–12 classrooms?

Into Your Classroom

How do I translate the research on cognitive load into my own classroom?

How will I know that this promising principle or practice had an impact on my learners?

LEARNING INTENTION

We are learning about cognitive load and how this concept impacts student learning.

SUCCESS CRITERIA

I will know we have successfully completed this module when

- I can describe what is meant by *cognitive load* on my learners.

- I can identify ways to manage the cognitive load of my learners that improve learning.

- I can develop specific ways to apply research on cognitive load in my classroom and evaluate the impact of this application.

WHAT IS COGNITIVE LOAD?

Cognitive load refers to the "weight" or "source of pressure" put on our students' working memory.

COGNITIVE LOAD REFERS TO THE "WEIGHT" OR "SOURCE OF PRESSURE" PUT ON OUR STUDENTS' WORKING MEMORY.

> Working memory is the component of memory where we hold attended-to information for a short time while we try to make sense of it. Working memory is also where much of our active cognitive processing actually occurs. For instance, it's where we think about the content of a lecture, analyze a textbook passage, or solve a problem. Basically, this is the component that does most of the mental work of the memory system—hence its name, working memory. (Ormrod, 2011, p. 186–187)

In our classrooms and with regard to how we and our students learn, one source of this "weight" or "pressure" on working memory comes from the declarative, procedural, and conditional knowledge we expect our students to know, understand, and do. Additional sources of "weight" or "pressure" can come from other interactions and experiences that learners are thinking about while also in our classrooms (e.g., an argument with a friend during lunch, the excitement of an after-school activity or event, the apprehension about a particular piece of content, or the anticipation of impending weather that may result in a day off from school). However, just as our electronic devices cannot handle unlimited amounts or an unlimited electrical load, our working memory, and thus our cognitive load, is limited. The quantity of information that can be actively processed in our working memory at one time is limited.

Let's demonstrate the limitations of our working memory with a quick experiment.

> Choose one of the following mathematics problems and solve the problem in your head:
>
> 1. 51,456 divided by 62
> 2. What is the value of x in $3x + 12 = 24$?
> 3. What are the coefficients of the following expanded polynomial: $(x + y)^3$?

Well, how did the experiment go? Without using paper or pencil, the previous problems were likely challenging, and you simply gave up and continued reading. Did you ever arrive at the correct answer for any of these problems? What was the difference between the problems you could do in your head and those that were too challenging? Use the space below to make a few notes about those differences. We will come back to these notes in just a moment.

There are three types of cognitive load: intrinsic, extrinsic, and germane (Sweller et al., 1998).

Intrinsic cognitive load refers to the overall difficulty and complexity of the specific content, skills, and understandings embedded in the learning experience or task. For example, solving a differential equation or analyzing the *Federalist Papers* in the secondary classroom. For younger learners, this might include adding and subtracting fractions with unlike denominators or reading Natalie Babbitt's *Tuck Everlasting*. The intrinsic load of a particular experience or task depends on the readiness of the learner and his or her interaction with content, skills, and understandings. But again, this type of cognitive load is related to the "intrinsic" nature of the topic.

For more resources related to three types of cognitive load, visit the companion website at resources.corwin.com/howlearningworks.

Use the space provided to list specific content, skills, and understandings that have a lot of intrinsic cognitive load. We can all list specific topics in our curricula that are just intrinsically difficult and complex for our learners. List them here and provide some explanation as to why you believe they are high intrinsic cognitive load topics.

Returning to the three mathematics problems on page 90, you can likely estimate the perceived level of intrinsic cognitive load from your perspective. In addition to the limitations of our working memory, the intrinsic cognitive load of each problem played a role in you arriving or not arriving at a solution.

Extrinsic cognitive load refers to the learning materials and the surrounding environment. Moving beyond the inherent nature of the topic, extrinsic cognitive load refers to the "packaging of the topic." For example, the complexity of the wording or phrasing of a question around a particular topic is extrinsic cognitive load. Had each of the three mathematics problems been embedded into a story or word problem that had difficult and complex vocabulary, the cognitive load of the tasks would have gone up for reasons above and beyond the nature of the mathematics. Similarly, asking young learners to make inferences and cite evidence from the text brings about a certain amount of intrinsic cognitive load. However, providing unclear examples or examples that are not developmentally appropriate adds additional extrinsic cognitive load.

Extrinsic cognitive load also includes distractions or factors within the learning environment that call for the learner to either attend to or deliberately ignore (e.g., other students' talking, a noise outside of the window, the temperature of the room, the proximity of snack time, lunch, or dismissal). Dealing with distractions adds to cognitive load.

THIS TYPE OF COGNITIVE LOAD IS RELATED TO THE "INTRINSIC" NATURE OF THE TOPIC.

Return to the earlier list of content, skills, and understandings that have a lot of intrinsic cognitive load. Now consider the learning materials and environment that surround the content, skills, and understandings. List specific characteristics or conditions that you believe add extrinsic cognitive load.

online resources

For more resources related to germane cognitive load, visit the companion website at resources.corwin.com/howlearningworks.

Germane cognitive load comes from learners engaging in the active processing of content, skills, and understandings through organizing, integrating, and connecting this learning with prior knowledge. This is the one we want! For learning by design to happen, we must monitor the level of intrinsic cognitive load in our learners, reduce the level of extrinsic cognitive load, and design learning experiences and tasks that maximize germane cognitive load. Germane cognitive load is the active engagement in learning experiences and tasks that leads to the acquisition, consolidation, and storage of declarative, procedural, and conditional learning. This includes many of the promising principles we have explored prior to this module.

Take a moment and in the space provided make an explicit connection between germane cognitive load and the previous promising principles. Flip back to the previous modules to provide specific examples of how they support our design in maximizing germane cognitive load.

Promising Principle	How Do They Support Our Design in Maximizing Germane Cognitive Load?
Motivation	
Attention	
Elaborate Encoding	
Retrieval and Practice	

Let's return one last time to the three mathematics problems, specifically, problems 2 and 3. To maximize germane cognitive load, we might provide opportunities that allow learners to discover and apply the patterns generated in Pascal's Triangle and the coefficients in an expanded binomial. Another way to enhance germane cognitive load is to provide opportunities for learners to see that $y = 3x + 12$ generates a line on which the ordered pair (4, 24) is a solution.

Now, let's link the concept of germane cognitive load with our work in previous modules. Return to your earlier list of content, skills, and understandings that have a lot of intrinsic cognitive load. List specific strategies or approaches that you can use to enhance the germane cognitive load for these topics. To help generate ideas, customize the ideas you developed around motivation, attention, elaborate encoding, and retrieval and practice.

Before moving into the implementation of cognitive load theory into your classroom, let's engage in retrieval and practice around the three types of cognitive load. Use the three-way Venn diagram to compare and contrast intrinsic, extrinsic, and germane cognitive load. Use specific examples from your own classroom—refer to the list you have already generated in the module to get started.

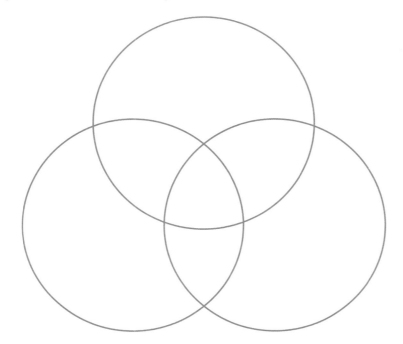

WHAT DOES THIS PRINCIPLE OR PRACTICE LOOK LIKE IN THE CLASSROOM?

Managing, minimizing, and maximizing the different types of cognitive load is paramount in learning by design. Just as a surge protector prevents overwhelming our devices with electricity, our cognitive architecture is set up to do the same thing with our working memory.

Intrinsic Load + Extraneous Load + Germane Load

Manage   **Minimize**   **Maximize**

Take a moment and flip back to Ormrod's definition of working memory on page 90. Please circle, underline, or highlight the following words:

attend

make sense

active cognitive processing

online resources

For more resources related to classroom practice guide related to cognitive load theory, visit the companion website at resources.corwin.com/howlearningworks.

To understand what the managing, minimizing, and maximizing of cognitive load looks like in our classrooms, we have to be clear about what we want our learners to attend to, make sense of, and actively process. Then, and only then, can we make intentional, purposeful, and deliberate decisions about cognitive load. Figure 9.2 shares some promising practices that are extracted from the research on cognitive load theory.

9.2 **EXTRACTING PROMISING PRINCIPLES AND PRACTICES FROM RETRIEVAL AND PRACTICE RESEARCH TO THE CLASSROOM**

Practice	Summary of What This Practice Looks Like in the Classroom	Classroom Example
Strive for Coherence	Remove any unnecessary and irrelevant information from the instructions, narratives, or descriptions of the learning materials.	In mathematics, ensure that the words and images contain only the information that is essential for the concept, skill, or application of that concept and skill.

Practice	Summary of What This Practice Looks Like in the Classroom	Classroom Example
Utilize Signaling	Utilize tools and techniques that direct learners' attention to the essential content, skills, and understandings.	In social studies, use fill-in notes that require learners to "fill in" the essential information during a learning experience. This may also include using **bold words**, *italics*, and other graphics.
Avoid Redundancy	When using graphics, avoid providing text and audio at the same time. This requires the learner to simultaneously process redundant pieces of information.	When using graphics (e.g., science or art history), explain the image or graphic with a verbal or audio explanation *or* text. Do not use both at the same time.
Place Labels and Descriptors Close to Graphics	Often referred to as *spatial contiguity*, place labels and descriptors right next to the location on the image or graphic they are referring to.	In a diesel mechanic class, the manual for basic care and maintenance should have labels right next to the parts and processes in the manual. Color coding the images and providing a legend is not effective.
Present Labels and Descriptors at the Same Time as the Graphics	This practice is referred to as temporal contiguity. The labels, descriptors, and the image or graphic should be presented at the same time.	When teaching learners about text features, the text feature, along with the name, is presented at the same time. This links the image and the term together.

HOW DO WE IMPLEMENT THIS PRINCIPLE AND PRACTICE INTO OUR CLASSROOMS?

Use the next pages to map out your challenge or problem of practice. You can return to Figure 9.2 for examples of alleviating cognitive load in your classroom that you might want to focus on in this module.

Challenge or Problem of Practice:

What evidence do you have that this is a challenge or problem of practice with your learners (e.g., observations, conversations, entrance tickets, exit tickets, attendance data, assignment submission)?

Describe the promising principle or practice you want to use.

Link the promising principle or practice to research from the science of learning on cognitive load. Refer back to the previous information in this module, if necessary.

Describe, in as much detail as possible, how you will implement this promising principle or practice. Again, refer back to Figure 9.2 for examples.

How will you collaborate with your accountability partner, instructional coach, or PLC+ team to determine if your promising principle or practice worked? What evidence would convince you and your colleagues that the principle or practice did not work?

»» Checks for Understanding

Take a moment and return to the success criteria for this module. As you have done in the previous modules, respond to the following questions by "showing what you know."

Know	Show (Generate a response to the question that "shows what you know")
Can I describe what is meant by *cognitive load* on my learners?	
Can I identify ways to manage the cognitive load of my learners that improve learning?	
Can I develop specific ways to apply research on cognitive load in my classroom and evaluate the impact of this application?	

We now turn our attention to productive struggle.

10

PROMISING PRINCIPLE 6: PRODUCTIVE STRUGGLE

Before addressing the idea of productive struggle, which seems like a paradox in learning, let's step back and frame the conversation of this module using earth and space science. Astronomers and astrobiologists have long sought to discover other planetary bodies that either contained life or possessed the necessary conditions to sustain life. This pursuit in earth and space science is the inspiration for some pretty awesome movies. But we digress. In 1913, astronomer Edward Maunder introduced the concept of a circumstellar habitable zone, simply referred to as the habitable zone. The habitable zone is the range of orbits around a star within which planets have the necessary conditions to support liquid water (see Lorenz, 2020).

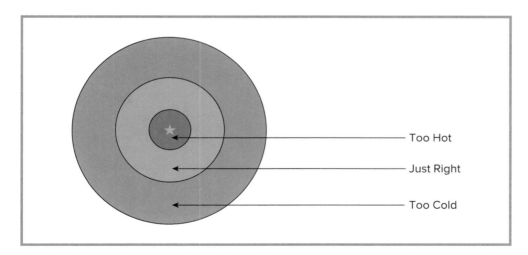

In other words, the distance between the star and the planets is not too hot, not too cold, but just right for liquid water. And, as you have already guessed, another name for the habitable zone is the Goldilocks Zone. While the Goldilocks Zone was originally developed to describe the conditions on planetary objects, this same idea can be applied to the learning experiences or tasks in our schools and classrooms.

Let's revise Edward Maunder's original concept to help us better understand the concept of productive struggle. If the center of the concentric circles was revised to be a learning task or experience, how would you revise the descriptors of the three areas beyond the learning task or experience?

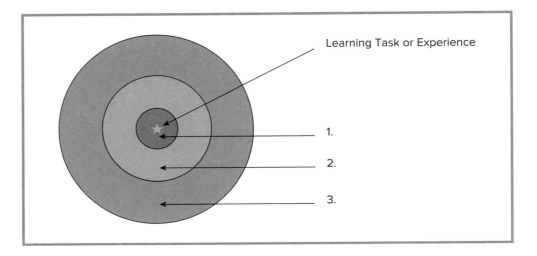

As we have noted, three types of student learning are in focus in this playbook: declarative, procedural, and conditional. We have to plan, design, and implement tasks and experiences that provide students with opportunities to acquire, consolidate, and store this learning, as well as the flexibility to return to different aspects of the learning when necessary (e.g., additional encoding, retrieval and practice, cognitive load challenges). The level of struggle in each learning task or experience matters as students move forward in their learning. Thus, to provide tasks and experiences that fall within the Goldilocks Zone (i.e., productive struggle), we have to balance the difficulty and complexity experienced by each of our students. In other words, the task or experience cannot be too hard and not too boring. Productive struggle is a promising principle of how we learn (see Figure 10.1).

10.1 A FRAMEWORK FOR TRANSLATING THE SCIENCE OF LEARNING ON PRODUCTIVE STRUGGLE INTO A PROMISING PRINCIPLE OR PRACTICE

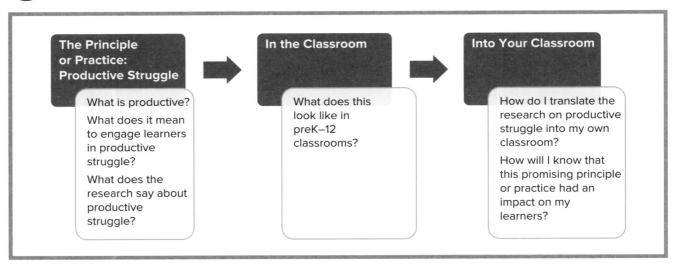

LEARNING INTENTION

We are learning about productive struggle and how to engage learners in this type of struggle improves student learning.

SUCCESS CRITERIA

I will know we have successfully completed this module when

- I can compare and contrast *productive* and *unproductive struggle*.

- I can describe how to engage learners in struggle that improves learning.

- I can develop specific ways to apply research on productive struggle in my classroom and evaluate the impact of this application.

Let's revisit an earlier sentence regarding productive struggle:

To provide tasks and experiences that fall within the Goldilocks Zone, we have to balance the difficulty and complexity experienced by each of our students.

Circle, underline, or highlight specific words or phrases that grab your attention in the above sentence. The implications of this statement on learning by design cannot be overlooked. Use the space provided to develop some questions you have after rereading the above sentence.

These questions will help us focus on the next part of this module. For example, you may have written down questions like

1. What is productive struggle?

2. Is this different for every learner?

3. What is the difference between difficulty and complexity?

We will tackle these three questions and more.

WHAT IS PRODUCTIVE STRUGGLE?

Productive struggle occurs when the complexity and difficulty of the task or experience are challenging enough so that the learner must devote significant cognitive resources to make progress in that task or experience, but is provided the necessary supports and scaffolds to prevent frustration or discouragement. Barbara Blackburn describes productive struggle as the learner's sweet spot (Blackburn, 2018). Whether you prefer the learner's sweet spot or operating within the Goldilocks Zone, productive struggle means different things to different learners. For example, what is complex for one learner may not be as complex for another. What is difficult for some students may not be as difficult for others. Being clear about what is meant by complexity and difficulty is the first step in finding the Goldilocks Zone for our learners. Use the space below to create your own definitions or descriptions of complexity and difficulty. What do you think these two terms mean?

PRODUCTIVE STRUGGLE MEANS DIFFERENT THINGS TO DIFFERENT LEARNERS.

Complexity	Difficulty

Complexity describes the level of thinking required to engage in the learning task or experience. For example, identifying author's craft or purpose is less cognitively complex than comparing and contrasting two pieces of writing across multiple elements—especially if both pieces of writing are new to the learners. Similarly, analyzing a historical document for purpose, message, and audience represents greater cognitive complexity than describing the document.

Complexity = Thinking

Difficulty, then, describes the amount of effort required to engage in the learning task or experience, accomplish the task, and meet the expected learning intention and success criteria. Responding to 25 questions about a text passage contains a greater degree of difficulty than responding to one or two questions. Likewise, working on three or four multistep mathematics problems is less difficult than working through 30 multistep mathematics problems, saying nothing about the complexity of the task.

Difficulty = Effort

Take a moment and return to your original definitions or descriptions of complexity and difficulty. What edits or revisions would you make to your first response?

The tasks and experiences that we plan, design, and implement to move learning forward can be described in terms of both complexity and difficulty. In response to the question *How do we learn?,* the answer is productive struggle. When both difficulty and complexity are high, students are likely to struggle—and struggle is important to the learning process. That's not to say that all tasks and experiences should be a struggle for students all the time, but rather that teachers should strategically place students in situations that require struggle so that they can extend their learning.

Look back at the previous module on cognitive load. How does our learners' cognitive load guide and inform our decisions about productive struggle? Use the space provided to write down "things to consider" when determining the limitations of learners engaged in productive struggle?

Look back even farther at the previous modules on attention and motivation. How does the research on attention and motivation inform our decisions about productive struggle? Use the space provided to write down "things to consider" when determining the limitations of learners engaged in productive struggle?

As we translate the promising principle of productive struggle into practice, one area of concern that may be on your mind is failure.

As Kapur (2008) noted, productive failure is an important consideration in effective learning. Kapur (2014) further observed, "Learning from mistakes, errors, and failure seems intuitive and compelling. Everyone can relate to it. But if failure is a powerful learning mechanism, why do we wait for it to happen? Why can't we design for it, understand how and when it works? What if designing for failure while learning a new concept or skill could result in more robust learning?" (para. 1). For example, learners in a high school physics class are working on an open-ended problem that asks them to consider how the starting height and initial velocity of an object influence the projectile motion of that object. They are provided multiple supplies (e.g., objects of different masses, plastic tracking, measuring devices), but they are asked to design their own experiments to answer the question. This is both a difficult and a complex task.

When students are engaged in productive struggle, they must constantly monitor their conversations and progress toward completing the task or experiences; this allows us to both identify a struggle and then determine what caused the struggle. Only then can we identify appropriate "next steps" to reduce the cognitive overload as learners move forward in that task or experience. This monitoring and purposeful intervention allows teachers to engage learners in self-reflection, self-monitoring, and self-evaluation, which requires additional practice and feedback to attain mastery, or fluency. We will unpack *feedback* in the next module, so keep this aspect of productive struggle in your working memory. To ensure you do not experience cognitive overload, please flip forward to the next module and write the words "Productive Struggle" at the top of the page.

Productive struggle is important to how we learn, but students also require opportunities to engage in retrieval and practice if they are going to develop proficiency or mastery in specific declarative, procedural, or conditional learning.

Look back at the previous module on retrieval and practice. Use the space provided to write down "things to consider" when learners are engaged in productive struggle. What does this have to do with retrieval and practice?

Using struggles to guide subsequent tasks and experiences offers learners the opportunity to engage in retrieval and practice. For example, if the struggle in the previously mentioned physics class becomes unproductive (i.e., decreased attention, motivation, and cognitive overload) because our learners do not have the prior knowledge or background knowledge necessary for understanding the relationship between horizontal and vertical motion in projectiles, we must provide additional learning tasks and experiences. As you remember from Module 3, there are other reasons that struggle becomes unproductive (Chew & Cerbin, 2020):

1. Learners may hold specific beliefs or have specific attitudes about a particular subject or content area.

2. Learners may not *yet* have the skills for self-reflection, self-monitoring, and self-evaluation.

3. Learners may have a fear about a particular class that may stem from a mistrust of the teacher.

4. Learners may not have the necessary prior knowledge or background knowledge to engage in productive struggle (e.g., unproductive struggle and unproductive failure).

5. Learners may have misconceptions about the topic or specific content of the task or experience.

6. Learners may not have the most effective learning strategies for engaging in productive struggle.

7. Learners may not transfer previous learning to a new task or experience.

8. Learners may not pay attention and notice the necessary aspects of the task or experience to successfully navigate the struggle.

9. Learners may experience cognitive overload while engaging in the task or experience.

The challenges to learning by design will significantly impact learners' willingness to and capacity for engaging in productive struggle. As we design tasks and experiences that incorporate productive struggle, we have to use the evidence that we generate and gather about student learning. Before moving forward, flip back to your work in Module 3 on page 35 and review your plan for how you will generate and gather evidence for each challenge. Make edits, revisions, or add new ideas to your plan. We will put this plan into action in the next section of this playbook. For now, let's look at productive struggle in action.

WHAT DOES THIS PRINCIPLE OR PRACTICE LOOK LIKE IN THE CLASSROOM?

Productive struggle is about the quality of the learning task or experience, not the quantity. This means we must intentionally, deliberately, and purposefully design our tasks and experiences to include elements that enhance the quality for all learners based on what they need to move their learning forward. Some ideas include but are not limited to

→ Access to complex text

→ A focus on extracting and leveraging evidence from text to explain thinking

→ The opportunity to build background knowledge through informational text

→ A balance between declarative, procedural, and conditional learning

→ Integrating the above elements across the disciplines

To look further into the application of productive struggle in the classroom, we want to address what it is *not*—the misconceptions about productive struggle (see Figure 10.2).

10.2 MISCONCEPTIONS ABOUT PRODUCTIVE STRUGGLE

Misconception	Explanation
An abundance of homework or tasks expected to be completed outside of the classroom provides productive struggle.	Oftentimes, we falsely believe that providing an abundance of "things" for learners to do at home with their parents, guardians, or caregivers is promoting productive struggle. This promotes inequity for learners that do not have access to necessary resources outside of school.
More content is better.	The coverage of more topics, tasks, and/or activities does not represent productive struggle. This misconception sometimes leads to expecting learners to engage with content, skills, and knowledge that they are not ready for yet.
Not all of our learners can handle productive struggle.	Productive struggle is often set aside for certain learners that we perceive are capable of handling it. Statements like "my students can't do that" exemplify this misconception. This reflects deficit thinking and denies some learners the access and opportunity to the highest level of learning.
Scaffolding and support lessen the impact of productive struggle.	The task or experience does not have to be completed independently and without any help to be a productive struggle. In fact, the opposite is true. This misconception perpetuates the internal belief of learners that "I should not ask for help." Scaffolding and supporting are essential components of all learning, for all learners.
Curricula and programs provide productive struggle.	We often assume that the resources we are provided incorporate productive struggle. Although this is not an unfair expectation, this is a misconception. We must analyze the tasks and experiences within our available resources to make the necessary adaptations for the local context of our classroom. Those curriculum writers and program developers don't know our students as well as we do.
Standards of learning create productive struggle.	Remember, standards tell us what to teach, not how. Productive struggle represents the "how" and should be informed by the "who." The "who" in this case are our learners. Simply put, standards do not automatically provide productive struggle, they create expectations for learning. Productive struggle comes by design.

Source: Adapted from Blackburn (2018).

HOW DO WE IMPLEMENT THIS PRINCIPLE AND PRACTICE INTO OUR CLASSROOMS?

Use the space below to map out your challenge or problem of practice. You can return to Figure 10.2 for examples of productive struggle in your classroom that you might want to focus on in this module.

Challenge or Problem of Practice:

What evidence do you have that this is a challenge or problem of practice with your learners (e.g., observations, conversations, entrance tickets, exit tickets, attendance data, assignment submission)?

Describe the promising principle or practice you want to use.

Link the promising principle or practice to research from the science of learning on productive struggle. Refer back to the previous information in this module, if necessary.

Describe, in as much detail as possible, how you will implement this promising principle or practice. Again, refer back to Figure 10.2 for examples.

How will you collaborate with your accountability partner, instructional coach, or PLC+ team to determine if your promising principle or practice worked? What evidence would convince you and your colleagues that the principle or practice did not work?

 ## Checks for Understanding

Take a moment and return to the success criteria for this module. As you have done in the previous modules, respond to the following questions by "showing what you know."

Know	Show (Generate a response to the question that "shows what you know")
Can I compare and contrast productive and unproductive struggle?	
Can I describe how to engage learners in struggle that improves learning?	
Can I develop specific ways to apply research on productive struggle in my classroom and evaluate the impact of this application?	

Productive struggle requires effective feedback. It needs feedback at the right time, in the right amount, and through the right modality to move learning forward. We turn our attention to feedback before focusing on building learners' capacity to leverage the science of how they learn to take ownership of their own learning.

11

PROMISING PRINCIPLE 7: FEEDBACK

Feedback is the glue that holds the acquisition, consolidation, and storage of learning together. As learners progress in their learning journey, they acquire valuable information about how that journey is progressing. In addition, they must have the opportunity to share feedback about what is and what is not moving their learning forward. As we move into our final module and promising principle, we want to emphasize that the promising practice of feedback is not a one-way practice. Research from the science of learning on feedback suggests that the giving *and* receiving of feedback is essential in amplifying learning (see Figure 11.1).

11.1 A FRAMEWORK FOR TRANSLATING THE SCIENCE OF LEARNING ON FEEDBACK INTO A PROMISING PRINCIPLE OR PRACTICE

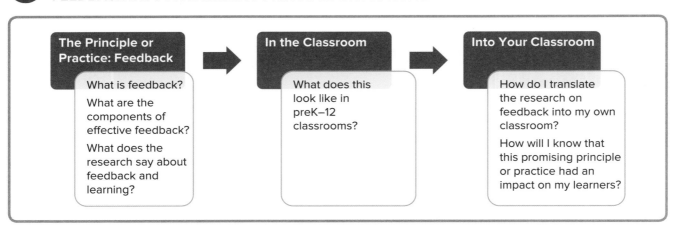

The Principle or Practice: Feedback

What is feedback?

What are the components of effective feedback?

What does the research say about feedback and learning?

In the Classroom

What does this look like in preK–12 classrooms?

Into Your Classroom

How do I translate the research on feedback into my own classroom?

How will I know that this promising principle or practice had an impact on my learners?

LEARNING INTENTION

We are learning about the role of feedback in moving learning forward.

SUCCESS CRITERIA

I will know we have successfully completed this module when

- I can describe the characteristics and components of effective feedback.

- I can explain the reciprocal nature of effective feedback in my classroom.

- I can develop specific ways to enhance the giving and receiving of feedback and evaluating the impact on my students' learning.

WHAT IS FEEDBACK AND WHAT MAKES IT EFFECTIVE?

Feedback is defined as the exchange of evaluative or corrective information about an action, event, or process and is the basis for improvement (Merriam-Webster, 2021c). This exchange of information provides support for learners as they direct their time, energy, and effort toward encoding, retrieval, and struggle. Feedback also supports learners in managing the cognitive load (more on this in the upcoming modules). Feedback only supports learning when the information is received and effectively integrated into the learning experience or task. To effectively integrate feedback into learning, the feedback must be received by the learner. To increase the likelihood that feedback is received and has an impact on increasing learning, feedback must address three very important questions for both the teacher and the learners (Hattie, 2012):

1. Where are we going?

2. How are we going?

3. Where do we go next?

Recall several exchanges of feedback between you and your learners. Did your learners integrate the feedback into their learning? If not, use the three questions above and jot down some possible reasons with your feedback that may not have been received and integrated into the learning experience or task.

1.

2.

3.

4.

As we mentioned in the opening of this module, the science of learning on feedback suggests that the giving and receiving of feedback is essential in amplifying learning. What opportunities do your learners have to share feedback about what is and what is not moving their learning forward? How does this show up in each of the other promising principles and practices? Use the chart below to write down how your learners give you feedback. The first one is done for you as an example.

Promising Principle or Practice	Ways Learners Give Feedback
Motivation	**My learners do not sustain their engagement in the science laboratory; they did not complete the questions at the end of the laboratory; they did not discuss the underlying science phenomenon.**
Attention	
Elaborate Encoding	
Retrieval and Practice	
Cognitive Load	
Productive Struggle	

Feedback has a powerful impact on learning. For feedback to work, we and our learners must have clarity about

➔ The expectations of the learning experience or task

➔ The current level of performance (the learners)

➔ Actions that we and our learners can take to close the gap.

The giving and receiving of feedback are designed to close the gap between learners' current level of declarative, procedure, and conditional knowledge and the expectations of where learners are going next in their learning journey. It is given to learners so that they know where to go next in their learning and is received by us to make decisions about where to go next in our instruction. Then, the feedback given and received should specifically target what learners are expected to say and do to demonstrate that they have met the expectations of the learning experience or task (i.e., learning intentions and success criteria). This feedback should be customized to support learners in closing the gap between their current level of declarative, procedural, and conditional learning and the expectations. And finally, this feedback should provide insight into where deliberate practice is needed to move learning forward.

Let's look at four specific examples of learning intentions and success criteria. These provide clarity about the expectations of the learning experience or task. Use the space provided to describe the focus of the feedback.

Learning Intentions	Examples of Success Criteria	Focus of the Feedback
Mathematics		
We are learning about the role of irrational numbers within the number system.	We can compare and contrast rational and irrational numbers. We can use a number line and benchmark rational numbers to model the approximate location of irrational numbers on a number line.	
Science		
I am learning about energy transfer in matter.	I can describe how matter changes from one form to another. I can use a phase diagram to explain the processes of state changes.	
English Language Arts		
I am learning about the relationship between author's purpose and author's craft.	I can describe the difference between author's purpose and author's craft. I can identify examples in my reading. I can explain the significance of my examples.	
Social Studies		
We are learning about the contributions of Muslim scholars and their impact on later civilizations.	We can describe contributions from Muslim scholars in the areas of science and medicine. We can describe contributions from Muslim scholars in the areas of philosophy, art, and literature. We can describe contributions from Muslim scholars in the area of mathematics.	

WHAT DOES THIS PRINCIPLE OR PRACTICE LOOK LIKE IN THE CLASSROOM?

We have looked at the definition of feedback and guidelines for how to decide what feedback to give and receive. Let's turn our attention to what this giving and receiving would look like in the classroom (see Figure 11.2). There are two main features of effective feedback that allow us to translate this promising principle into a promising practice.

For more resources related to feedback, visit the companion website at resources.corwin.com/howlearningworks.

online resources

1. **Focus on learning, not the individual**. Effective feedback should focus on the learning and not on the individual participating in the learning. Here's an example: "My explanation of energy transfer in the water cycle needs improving, not me as a person. My solution to the mathematics problem is wrong, but I am not a wrong person. My writing is not clear, but I am not a bad writer. My understanding of the historical timeline is fuzzy, but I am not stupid."

2. **Feedback also needs to come at the right time, personalized for the specific learner and their learning, and focus on moving learning forward.**

3. **Feedback should vary in terms of timing, amount, mode, and audience** (see Brookhart, 2008).

11.2 EXTRACTING PROMISING PRINCIPLES AND PRACTICES FROM FEEDBACK RESEARCH TO THE CLASSROOM

Feedback Strategies Can Vary in Terms of . . .	In These Ways . . .	Examples and Things to Consider
Timing	• When the feedback is given • How often feedback is given	• Provide immediate feedback for content (right/wrong). • Delay feedback slightly for more mathematical practices and science and engineering practices. • Never delay feedback beyond when it would make a difference in students' learning in the moment. • Provide feedback as often as is practical for all processes, tasks, and products.
Amount	• How many feedback points? • How much information in each point?	• Focus on those points that are directly related to the success criteria. • Choose those points that are essential for closing the gap. • Take into account the developmental stage of the learner (e.g., kindergarteners compared to high school seniors).
Mode	• Oral • Written • Visual/demonstration	• Select the best mode for the message. • When possible, it is best to engage in dialogue and questioning with the learner. • Give written feedback on written work. • Use teacher or student modeling if "how to do something" is an issue or if the student needs an example.
Audience	• Individual • Group/class	• Individual feedback says, "The teacher values my learning." • Group/class feedback works if most of the learners need the feedback. If not, group/class feedback is not effective. • Would it suffice to make a comment when passing the learners as they work on a problem or experiment? • Is a one-on-one conference better for providing feedback?

Let's look at specific examples of each of the variables in feedback to begin to see how this would translate into our classrooms. Consider the following scenarios in Figure 11.3. With your colleagues, identify which one is more effective and why.

11.3 **COMPARING TWO DIFFERENT APPROACHES TO GIVING AND RECEIVING FEEDBACK IN ENGLISH LANGUAGE ARTS AND SOCIAL STUDIES**

Option 1	Option 2	Why?
An elementary teacher reads student writing samples and identifies common errors. She plans whole class instruction on the use of reasons to support opinions because nearly every student in the class has neglected to do so. She also plans small group lessons for students who had other errors in their writing, including tense, subject-verb agreement, or the lack of a clear opinion.	The teacher reads student work and provides written feedback to students. Students are expected to review the feedback and revise their papers accordingly.	
A history teacher uses an online game to quiz students. He displays a question and students select their response on their mobile phones. He then shows them the number of students who selected each option, asking them to talk with their partners about the data. He then invites students to respond to the question again before showing them the correct answer and asking them to discuss why the incorrect answers are not appropriate.	A history teacher gives a weekly quiz on Fridays, and students receive their results on Mondays. They take a cumulative test at the end of the unit.	

The key difference between each of the four examples is the availability of timely feedback about the students' learning. Option 1 in each of the two examples suggests that the teacher was setting up the learning experience for learners to give and receive feedback at multiple points. These multiple points are identified by the success criteria. In other words, the teachers in Option 1 offered the opportunity to give and receive feedback as learners progressed from one success criterion to the next. Information about learners' performance within a specific timeframe allows them to use the information for adjusting their pathway toward declarative, procedural, and conditional learning. This supports where they should focus their attention, seek to elaborately encode, and engage in deliberate practice. Without timely information, learners cannot know where to go next and often continue moving forward, even if they are going in the wrong direction (see Figure 11.4).

11.4 COMPARING TWO DIFFERENT APPROACHES TO GIVING AND RECEIVING FEEDBACK IN MATHEMATICS AND SCIENCE

Option 1	Option 2	Why?
A teacher confers with students as they work on a problem-solving set of rational expressions. He asks individual students and pairs of students what they are working on. Listening to the students' thinking allows him to make a decision about how to respond in that moment. The teacher refers to his planned questions, anticipated student strategies, and the success criteria to choose his response.	A teacher collects a problem-solving set on rational expressions. He marks which answers are not correct and returns the problem-solving set to learners at the end of the week.	
A teacher marks the incorrect solutions in a problem-solving set on balancing equations and returns the set to learners at the end of the week. She asks them to partner up and identify where they made mistakes in each incorrect solution. They are to describe, in their own words, how they would solve the problem differently in the future.	A teacher returns a problem-solving set on balancing equations to learners at the end of the week. She informs the students that these problems will be on the final test and they should review this set before taking the test.	

Effective feedback must be specific about what additional steps will close the gap between where learners are and where they are going.

Take a moment and recall the three questions associated with effective feedback. You can look back to the beginning of this module if necessary.

> 1.
>
> 2.
>
> 3.

Comparing and contrasting the above examples, Option 1 provides specific information to learners that relates to declarative, procedural, and conditional learning. Learners could use the information in Option 1 to identify how they were going and where they needed to go next in their learning. Students then have information that allows them to mind the learning gap. In addition, Option 1 is constructive in nature. By being constructive, feedback serves a very useful purpose: *moving learning forward*. If the goal in each of our schools and classrooms is growth and achievement in learning, constructive feedback supports students as they progress in their learning. Growth implies that all of our students may not be where they need to be today, but they are farther along today than they were yesterday. Constructive feedback makes the journey about learning, not the individual.

HOW DO WE IMPLEMENT THIS PRINCIPLE AND PRACTICE INTO OUR CLASSROOMS?

Use the space below to map out your challenge or problem of practice. You can return to Figures 11.2, 11.3, and 11.4 for examples of the giving and receiving of effective feedback in your classroom that you might want to focus on in this module. In the upcoming modules, we will explore how to incorporate peer-to-peer feedback. For now, let's focus on giving and receiving feedback between us and our learners.

CONSTRUCTIVE FEEDBACK MAKES THE JOURNEY ABOUT LEARNING, NOT THE INDIVIDUAL.

Challenge or Problem of Practice:

What evidence do you have that this is a challenge or problem of practice with your learners (e.g., observations, conversations, entrance tickets, exit tickets, attendance data, assignment submission)?

Describe the promising principle or practice you want to use.

Link the promising principle or practice to research from the science of learning on feeback. Refer back to the previous information in this module, if necessary.

Describe, in as much detail as possible, how you will implement this promising principle or practice. Again, refer back to Figure 11.2 for examples.

How will you collaborate with your accountability partner, instructional coach, or PLC+ team to determine if your promising principle or practice worked? What evidence would convince you and your colleagues that the principle or practice did not work?

>>> Checks for Understanding

Take a moment and return to the success criteria for this module. As you have done in the previous modules, respond to the following questions by "showing what you know."

Know	Show (Generate a response to the question that "shows what you know")
Can I describe the characteristics and components of effective feedback?	
Can I explain the reciprocal nature of effective feedback in my classroom?	
Can I develop specific ways to enhance the giving and receiving of feedback and evaluating the impact on my students' learning?	

WHERE TO NEXT?

Over the past seven modules, we have explored seven promising principles and translated them into potential and promising practices in our classrooms. Each module offered opportunities to adapt these practices for use in your classroom, the local context. Furthermore, the successful implementation of these promising practices is driven by us and our students gathering evidence of impact on learning. With that being said, we are now going to make a major transition in this playbook. Starting with the next module, we will begin to explore how to build the capacity and efficacy of our students as they move beyond the specific learning experiences and outside of our classrooms. We want our students to take ownership of their learning and know what to do to move their learning forward when we are no longer their teacher. Return to page 6 in the introduction of this playbook. Building capacity and efficacy in our students through the explicit teaching of learning strategies supports learners by the following:

> Retrieve the four characteristics of self-regulated learners.
>
> 1.
>
> 2.
>
> 3.
>
> 4.

Here we go!

PART III

In this section:

12

EXPLICIT STRATEGY INSTRUCTION

Do our learners know what to do when they don't know what to do, and we are not around? This question serves as the impetus for the remaining modules of the playbook. One of the most exciting findings from the growing body of research on teaching and learning is that "when students become their own teachers, they exhibit the self-regulatory attributes that seem most desirable for learners: self-monitoring, self-evaluation, self-assessment, and self-teaching" (Hattie, 2012, p. 14). For our learners to become their own teachers, they must develop the characteristics of an assessment-capable learner (Frey et al., 2018).

> **FOR OUR LEARNERS TO BECOME THEIR OWN TEACHERS, THEY MUST DEVELOP THE CHARACTERISTICS OF AN ASSESSMENT-CAPABLE LEARNER.**

Assessment-capable learners

1. **Know their current level of understanding.** They are aware of what they already know, understand, and are able to do and what is going to be challenging for them to learn.

2. **Know where they are going next in their learning and are ready to take on the challenge.** They are clear about the learning intention, success criteria, and the expectations of the task or experience. They have the self-efficacy to persist in the face of a challenge.

3. **Select the right tools to help move their learning forward.** They have effective learning strategies and know when to use them. They also know what to do when they "get stuck."

4. **Seek feedback and recognize that errors are opportunities for learning.** They ask for feedback from both us and their peers, integrating that feedback into their learning.

5. **Monitor their learning progress, making adjustments when necessary.** They use the learning intentions, success criteria, expectations of the task or experience, and feedback to make decisions about where to go next in their learning.

6. **Recognize their learning and support their peers in their learning progression.** They learn from their peers and teach their peers when they need additional learning.

Take a moment and reflect on these six characteristics. Using the space provided, where are your learners in their journey to assessment capability?

	What Does This Mean in My Classroom?	Where Are My Learners in This Part of the Journey?
1. Know their current level of understanding.		
2. Know where they are going next in their learning and are ready to take on the challenge.		
3. Select the right tools to help move their learning forward.		
4. Seek feedback and recognize that errors are opportunities for learning.		
5. Monitor their learning progress, making adjustments when necessary.		
6. Recognize their learning and support their peers in their learning progression.		

Although each of these characteristics is essential in students developing into self-regulating learners, one of these will serve as the focus for the remaining modules of this playbook. Please circle, highlight, or underline number 3. *The promising principles and practices unpacked in the previous modules should not just be done to our students. We should explicitly teach learners how to use effective learning techniques in their own individual learning.* Again, we want our learners to know what to do when they don't know what to do, and we are not around!

LEARNING INTENTION

We are learning about the specific strategies that support student learning.

SUCCESS CRITERIA

I will know we have successfully completed this module when

- I can identify effective learning techniques that will support student learning.

- I can explain the role of gradual release of responsibility in explicit strategy instruction.

- I can evaluate the readiness of my learners for explicit strategy instruction.

WE SHOULD EXPLICITLY TEACH LEARNERS HOW TO USE EFFECTIVE LEARNING TECHNIQUES IN THEIR OWN INDIVIDUAL LEARNING.

Take a moment and return to Module 1, page 20. As you may recall, you were asked to use the blank pie chart to color in the percentage that reflects your belief about the responsibility for learning that falls to the teacher and the percentage of responsibility for learning that falls to the student. The example provided was based on the belief that 90% of the responsibility falls to the teacher and 10% falls to the learner.

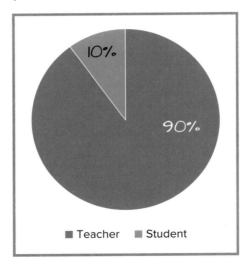

Let's revisit this in light of our own learning across the 12 modules. How would you divide up the responsibility for learning now? Color in and label your current belief.

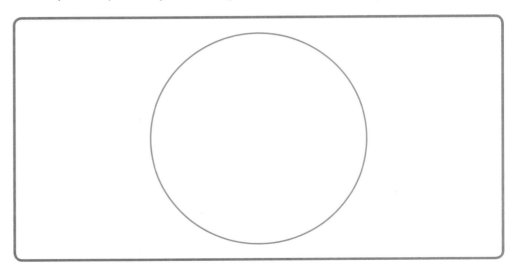

Did your response change from Module 1 to now? If so, why? If not, why not? Take a moment and add your reflection in the box below.

```
┌─────────────────────────────────────────────────────────────────┐
│                                                                   │
│                                                                   │
│                                                                   │
│                                                                   │
│                                                                   │
│                                                                   │
└─────────────────────────────────────────────────────────────────┘
```

THE GRADUAL RELEASE OF RESPONSIBILITY

Hopefully, the dividing up of responsibility is not all placed on us as the teacher. Instead, this proportion should change as learners develop proficiency in their self-monitoring, self-evaluation, self-assessment, and, finally, self-teaching. Early on in their learning journey, students will likely need more support and scaffolding in their learning. This is true in declarative, procedural, and conditional learning, as well as their selection of the right tools to move their learning forward.

Flip back to Module 3, pages 33 and 35. One significant barrier to learning is the use of ineffective learning strategies. Take a moment and review that particular barrier and practices for overcoming that barrier. Use the space below to write down your thoughts.

Ineffective Learning Strategies	Summarize This Particular Barrier in Your Own Words—Provide Some Examples From Your Own Classroom	Potential Practices for Overcoming This Barrier

12.1 GRADUAL RELEASE OF RESPONSIBILITY FOR STRATEGY INSTRUCTION

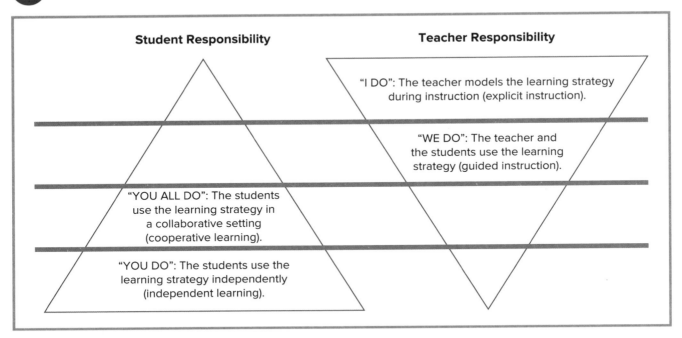

Source: Adapted from Fisher and Frey (2013).

For more resources related to ineffective learning strategies, visit the companion website at resources.corwin.com/howlearningworks.

To overcome ineffective learning strategies, we must explicitly teach learners how to use effective learning techniques in their own individual learning. However, this requires more than just "doing" promising practices in class. Learners must have opportunities to practice and reflect on the use of the practices to ultimately use them on their own. This is best done using the gradual release of responsibility (see Figure 12.1).

As you look over Figure 12.1, there are three key components that we would like you to add to this model.

Practice

Feedback

Shift in Responsibility

Please place those three components where you think they should go in Figure 12.1. Keep in mind, they may be placed in multiple locations.

Opportunities for practice and feedback drive the gradual release of responsibility and allow for the transition from one stage to the next. In other words, practice and feedback fill the space between "I DO," "WE DO," "YOU ALL DO," and "YOU DO." Only then will we experience the shift in responsibility that is most prominent between "WE DO" and "YOU ALL DO." This approach to explicit strategy instruction will drive our conversations over the next several modules. But before that, we must generate a list of practices that qualify as effective learning strategies or techniques. Based on how we learn, what learning strategies or techniques should we explicitly teach in our classrooms?

EFFECTIVE LEARNING PRACTICES

If asked, we could create a robust list of learning strategies. However, the effectiveness of each of the strategies on our list would vary. The science of how we learn has provided both promising principles and practices that allow us to look at learning strategies through the lens of what works best. Consider the following list of learning strategies. For each strategy, indicate whether you think that strategy is effective, ineffective, or unsure (e.g., don't know what the strategy is or does for learners).

Elaborative Interrogation	Effective	Ineffective	Unsure
Self-Explanation	Effective	Ineffective	Unsure
Summarization	Effective	Ineffective	Unsure
Highlighting	Effective	Ineffective	Unsure
Mnemonics	Effective	Ineffective	Unsure
Goal Setting	Effective	Ineffective	Unsure
Imagery	Effective	Ineffective	Unsure
Integrating Prior Knowledge	Effective	Ineffective	Unsure
Rereading	Effective	Ineffective	Unsure
Practice Testing	Effective	Ineffective	Unsure
Spaced Practice	Effective	Ineffective	Unsure
Concept Mapping	Effective	Ineffective	Unsure
Self-Teaching	Effective	Ineffective	Unsure
Self-Enacting	Effective	Ineffective	Unsure

We will unveil the answers as we move through the next several modules. For now, mark this page so that we can return to your responses as we unpack each one of these strategies. It's important to emphasize that research on how we learn has provided incredible insight into both classroom practices and strategies that support learners' attributes of self-regulation in learning. Our focus now is to take the promising principles from the previous modules and explicitly teach these strategies to our learners using the gradual release of responsibility.

For more resources related to strategies promoting generative learning, visit the companion website at resources.corwin.com/howlearningworks.

A RETURN TO GERMANE COGNITIVE LOAD

Before we transition out of this module and begin to look at individual learning strategies or techniques, we want to return to an earlier concept and explicitly link that concept to effective learning practices and the explicit instruction of those learning practices.

Learning can be activated or hindered if we are not cognizant of our learners' cognitive load. Take a moment and fill in the missing terms in the below image. If you find yourself "stuck," flip back to Module 9 for a quick review.

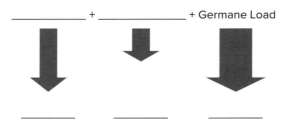

_____ + _____ + Germane Load

_____   _____   _____

Use the space provided and describe germane cognitive load.

Effective learning strategies and techniques that move learning forward maximize germane cognitive load. At the same time, those strategies must support learners' management of intrinsic cognitive load and their minimizing of extraneous cognitive load. If germane cognitive load comes from our learners engaging in the active processing of declarative, procedural, and conditional knowledge, our learning strategies must foster, nurture, and sustain that processing. Active, not passive. Generative, not repetitive. Fiorella and Mayer (2015) state

> . . . generative learning involves the learner engaging in appropriate cognitive processing during learning, including selecting relevant incoming material to attend to, organizing the material into a coherent cognitive structure in working memory, and integrating it with relevant prior knowledge activated from long-term memory. Learning is a generative activity when learners actively generate their own learning outcomes by interpreting what is presented to them rather than simply receiving it as presented. (p. viii)

online resources

For more resources related to study activities that foster generative learning, visit the companion website at resources.corwin.com/ howlearningworks.

As we close out this module and get ready for a closer look at learning strategies and techniques associated with attention and motivation, use this closing task to connect several concepts and ideas. On the next page, develop a connection between germane cognitive load, generative learning, and Wittrock's generative processes (see Module 7).

Summarize each concept in your own words (use specific examples to support your description)

Germane Cognitive Load	Generative Learning	Wittrock's Generative Processes

How are these three concepts similar?

How are these three concepts different?

Information on how we learn is not simply reserved for us as teachers. The promising practices generated from the promising principles of attention, motivation, elaborate encoding, retrieval and practice, cognitive load, productive struggle, and feedback can and should be explicitly taught to our students so that they can apply them to their own learning beyond our classroom. These are the tools that support the self-regulatory attributes of learners. Let's start with explicitly supporting learners in self-regulating their attention and motivation.

Checks for Understanding

Take a moment and return to the success criteria for this module. As you have done in the previous modules, respond to the following questions by "showing what you know." However, try something a bit different. Attach student work samples, comments, or feedback to support your responses.

Know	Show (Generate a response to the question that "shows what you know"; include student work samples, comments, or feedback)
Can I identify effective learning techniques that will support student learning?	
Can I explain the role of gradual release of responsibility in explicit strategy instruction?	
Can I evaluate the readiness of my learners for explicit strategy instruction?	

As a quick aside, have you noticed how we have modeled each of the principles and practices throughout the playbook? That is by design—more on that later.

13

LEARNING STRATEGY 1: GOAL SETTING

Motivating our students to engage in their learning, take ownership of their own progress, and then apply what they have learned beyond the walls of our classrooms is a key component in the science of how we learn. Each of the promising principles and practices in this playbook makes an implicit assumption about our students: that they are motivated learners. This observation is worth repeating; most studies in education, especially in the science of learning, assume a motivated learner. We know this is not always the case and thus devote time to motivating our students to engage, own, and apply their learning.

For more resources related to motivation, visit the companion website at resources.corwin.com/ howlearningworks.

Take a moment and retrieve the factors that contribute to the motivation of learners. Use the space below to record your thinking. If you need additional support, flip back to your work in Module 5.

The factors you listed above are likely factors that you have control over and implement in your classroom.

But remember, this part of the playbook is focusing on the explicit instruction of strategies that allow learners to exhibit the self-regulatory attributes that seem most desirable for learners: self-monitoring, self-evaluation, self-assessment, and self-teaching. In other words, how do we begin to transfer the responsibility of motivation from solely our responsibility as the teacher to the responsibility of the learner? One approach is to explicitly teach our students to set a learning goal, develop a plan for meeting that goal, and monitor their progress toward the goal.

The learning strategy in this module is **goal setting.**

LEARNING INTENTION

We are learning about goal setting and how it supports student learning.

SUCCESS CRITERIA

I will know we have successfully completed this module when

- I can describe the benefits of goal setting.

- I can explain how goal setting supports motivation along with the other promising principles.

- I can map out a process for implementing goal setting in my classroom.

THE BENEFITS OF GOAL SETTING

To move from being motivated to self-motivation, learners must

1. Tap into their own interests and passions

2. Believe that their efforts will pay off in both the short term and long term

3. Link their efforts to specific outcomes

4. Focus on developing competency, mastery, and deeper understanding

5. Be around other individuals who experience success from their efforts (Desender et al., 2016).

online resources

For more resources related to effort being contagious, visit the companion website at resources.corwin.com/howlearningworks.

Therefore, goal setting must focus on both the specific needs of the learners and the learners' interests and passions. For example, some goals might zero in on specific declarative, procedural, and conditional learning that the student needs to move forward in their learning (e.g., use a wider range of color in their artwork, include more details in their scientific arguments, provide more links between social, cultural, political, and economic characteristics in human geography, or develop a spaced-out study schedule for the upcoming mathematics test). Other goals may integrate students' interests and passions into their learning (e.g., selecting nonfiction texts based on a love of dolphins or U.S. presidents in a unit on text features).

Goal setting should also include opportunities for teacher and peer feedback so that learners have opportunities to reflect on, monitor, and evaluate their progress toward the goal. While goal setting is a major contributor to motivating our learners, this strategy will also support the application of the other principles and practices as well. Use the space provided to describe how you think goal setting benefits motivation, attention, elaborate encoding, retrieval and practice, cognitive load, productive struggle, and feedback. You may need to flip back to earlier modules. "Feedback" is done for you as an example.

GOAL SETTING

Motivation	
Attention	
Elaborate Encoding	
Retrieval and Practice	
Cognitive Load	
Productive Struggle	
Feedback	Effective feedback answers three questions for the learner (see Module 11): where am I going, how am I going, and where do I go next? The learners' goals clearly define the appropriate answers to these three questions for the teacher and peers giving feedback. The learners' goals, action plan, and monitoring allow learners to answer these three questions for themselves.

GETTING READY FOR GOAL SETTING

What makes a good goal? We have all set goals for ourselves that did absolutely nothing to motivate us or even prompt us to act out of obligation. We have also set goals that moved us to focus intently on the outcome, not out of obligation, but out of joy and excitement. What's the difference? Well, some goals are smart, others are not. Let us explain.

online resources

For more resources related to the original S.M.A.R.T. goal article and to motivation and knowing why, visit the companion website at resources.corwin.com/howlearningworks.

In 1981, George Doran introduced the acronym and concept of a S.M.A.R.T. goal. If you are like us, you are shocked that something so commonly referenced in schools and classrooms can be traced back to the source. For George Doran, he simply developed an acronym that supported the growth and development of a company. A S.M.A.R.T. goal, as pointed out by Doran (1981), "enabled an organization to focus on problems, and give the company a sense of direction . . . (p. 35)."

That's exactly what we want our learners to do: (1) focus on their learning; (2) provide a sense of direction about where and how to move forward in their learning. These are two important aspects of a goal. Students must know what it is they are aiming for and why this particular "aim" is important or is of value to the learner and their learning.

You likely noticed the addition of two letters, E and R. Since Doran's initial conceptualization of a S.M.A.R.T. goal, *evaluate* and *re-evaluate* have been added to the goal-setting process. Use the space below and explain why these two additional components are both necessary and important in the goal-setting process.

		Example
S: Specific	What is the specific declarative, procedural, and conditional learning outcome? For a goal to focus the learner on the "what" and "why" of learning, the goal must be directed toward a specific area needing improvement.	**Elementary School Mathematics:** I want to work on solving two-digit subtraction problems with regroup. **High School Social Studies:** I want to identify parallels between the Black Lives Matter Movement and the Civil Rights Movement.
M: Measurable	In addition to specific, a goal must be measurable so that learners can determine where they are in progress toward the goal.	**Elementary School Mathematics:** I will know I have met my goal when I am able to explain my solution, evaluate the reasonableness of my solution, and make revisions to my solution when I am not correct. **High School Social Studies:** I will know I have met my goal by developing a comparative essay of these two time periods.
A: Attainable and Ambitious	A goal must be challenging, yet realistic. Progress toward meeting the goal should involve productive struggle (see Module 10).	**Elementary School Mathematics:** I will choose the math center twice each week during center time. I will do this for three weeks. **High School Social Studies:** I will use my advisory period to devote time to this project. I will also meet with the School Media Specialist at the beginning and end of each week to ensure I have the necessary resources.
R: Reason	As mentioned above, the goal must focus on a specific need or interest.	**Elementary School Mathematics:** I want to get better at subtraction story problems because I had lots of questions about them during math block last week. **High School Social Studies:** I want to be more aware of issues related to diversity, equity, and inclusion in my own city.
T: Timely	There must be time restraints on the goal to support reflecting, refining, and reviewing of the goal.	**Elementary School Mathematics:** I will reach my goal by the end of the quarter. **High School Social Studies:** I will reach my goal by the end of the third week of this unit.
E: Evaluate	The goal must encourage monitoring, reflecting, and evaluating. There must be points for checking in to assess progress toward the goal.	**Elementary School Mathematics:** I will conference with my teacher once a week and have work samples to share with him. **High School Social Studies:** I have set up meetings with my social studies teacher twice a week to get feedback on my research and writing. I also have a classmate that has agreed to read my writing.
R: Re-Evaluate	Evaluation must be continuous. The goal must be re-evaluated during the process so that learners are able to make adjustments along the way.	**Elementary School Mathematics:** I will decide what problems to try next after each conference. **High School Social Studies:** I will make edits and revisions based on the feedback I receive from my teacher and classmate.

S.M.A.R.T.E.R. Goal

Name _____ **Date** _____

	Description	Teacher Feedback
S: Specific		
M: Measurable		
A: Attainable and Ambitious		
R: Reason		
T: Timely		
E: Evaluate		
R: Re-Evaluate		

Source: Adapted from Fisher et al. (2019).

THE PROCESS OF GOAL SETTING

Now that we have looked at the benefits of goal setting and unpacked what makes a good goal, let's develop the process for explicitly teaching this learning strategy to our students (see Figure 13.1).

13.1   THE GOAL-SETTING PROCESS

| Learners must first identify and unpack their goal using the S.M.A.R.T.E.R. acronym. | → | Learners develop a plan for action that will guide their progress toward meeting their goal. | → | Learners establish a timeline for reflecting, refining, and revising the goal. |

The template on the previous page provides a format for the first part of the goal-setting process. This template can be used as we gradually release the responsibility of goal setting to our learners. For example, we might begin by setting a class S.M.A.R.T.E.R. goal and explicitly teaching this part of the process. From there, the template can be used for collaborative and then individual S.M.A.R.T.E.R. goals (see Figure 13.2).

13.2   GRADUAL RELEASE OF RESPONSIBILITY FOR GOAL SETTING

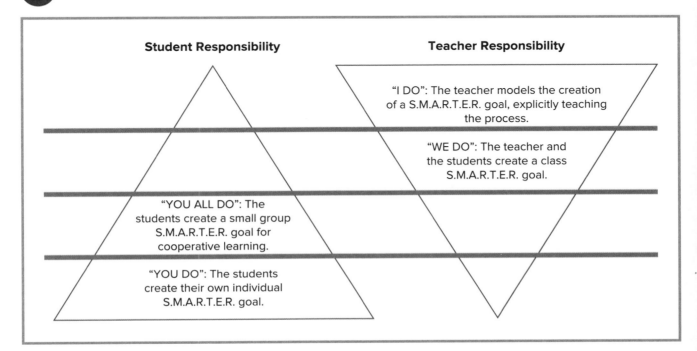

Source: Adapted from Fisher and Frey (2013).

Take a moment and map out how you will explicitly teach goal setting to your learners. Make sure to not only map out the gradual release of responsibility, but include a potential timeline for this release, opportunities for practice, and feedback. Start with when you want learners to independently develop their own S.M.A.R.T.E.R. goals and then walk it back. Use the space provided to accomplish this task.

The second part of the goal-setting process is the development of a plan for action. This includes, but is not limited to, an overview of the plan, identifying the necessary resources, and specific ways to monitor progress and evaluate that progress.

Overview of the Plan	This part of the plan for action should deconstruct the goal into small, measurable chunks that help learners believe that their efforts will pay off in both the short-term and long-term and link their efforts to specific outcomes.
Resources	Learners should first develop a list of resources they believe they will need during their work on the goal. However, this part of the plan will be revised frequently during the work toward the goal.
Progress Monitoring	This describes how and when progress will be monitored during the work toward the goal. Learners, in collaboration with their teachers, should specify these check-ins, what will specifically be done, and who will support them.
Evaluation	This part of the plan for action simply defines how the learner will evaluate their success and where to go next in his or her learning.

GOAL SETTING MUST FOCUS ON BOTH THE SPECIFIC NEEDS OF THE LEARNERS AND THE LEARNERS' INTERESTS AND PASSIONS.

The plan for action can be implemented using an interactive document or kept in the learners' portfolios, interactive notebooks, or personal files in the classroom. This plan is meant to be visited frequently and revised often. The template for this plan of action is meant to be implemented gradually, just like the creation of the S.M.A.R.T.E.R. goal.

PLAN FOR ACTION

Name _____   **Date** _____

Overview of the Plan	What are the specific steps to reaching my goal?
Resources	What resources do I need to support my learning and progress toward my goal?
Progress Monitoring	How will I monitor my progress toward my learning goal? Who will support that monitoring?
Evaluation	When and how will I evaluate my learning? What will the next steps be in my learning?

Source: Adapted from Fisher et al. (2019).

Take a moment and map out how you will explicitly teach learners to develop a plan of action. Again, start with when you want learners to independently develop their own plans for action and then walk it back. Use the space provided to accomplish this task. Be sure to include time for practice, feedback, and the shift in responsibility.

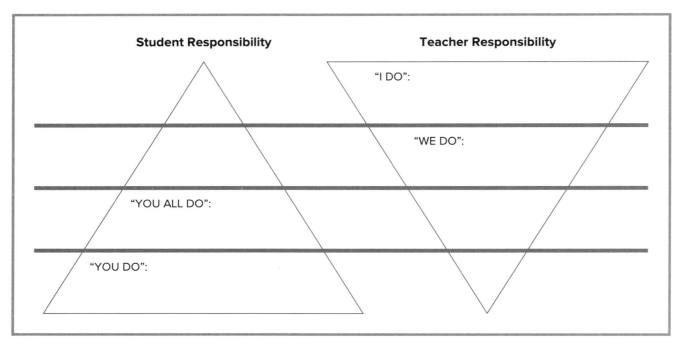

Source: Adapted from Fisher and Frey (2013).

The final part of the goal-setting process is the continual revising, refining, and revisiting of the goal. Returning to the table on page 133 of this module, goal setting incorporates other promising principles and practices. Elaborate encoding, retrieval and practice, cognitive load, productive struggle, and feedback are all components of this particular learning strategy. That is exactly why this is the first strategy we address in this playbook. Flip back to page 127 in Module 12. Make sure that you circled, underlined, or highlighted *effective* beside *goal setting*.

Much like the plan for action, this part of the goal-setting process can be implemented using an interactive document or kept in the learners' portfolios, interactive notebooks, or personal files in the classroom. This is also meant to be visited frequently and revised often.

Checks for Understanding

Take a moment and return to the success criteria for this module. As you have done in the previous modules, respond to the following questions by "showing what you know." Attach student work samples, comments, or feedback to support your responses.

Know	Show (Generate a response to the question that "shows what you know"; include student work samples, comments, or feedback)
Can I describe the benefits of goal setting?	
Can I explain how goal setting supports motivation along with the other promising principles?	
Can I map out a process for implementing goal setting in my classroom?	

14

LEARNING STRATEGY 2: INTEGRATING PRIOR KNOWLEDGE

Let's start this module off with a thought experiment. Imagine if someone arrived at your door with a reusable grocery bag containing the following items:

1. 1 dozen eggs

2. 7 coat hangers

3. A bag of mulch

4. The latest edition of your favorite magazine

5. A bar of soap

What would you do with these items if you had no choice but to accept and keep all of them? Be specific.

Now consider the following items from the standards of learning for high school World History (Virginia Department of Education, 2016):

1. Italy was the most commercially advanced, urbanized, literate area of high and later medieval Europe.

2. The remains of ancient Rome were most visible in Italy.

3. Italy's wealth, literacy, and pride in its Roman past provided the foundations of the Italian Renaissance.

4. Wealth accumulated from European trade with the Middle East led to the rise of Italian city-states. Wealthy merchants were active civic leaders.

5. Machiavelli observed city-state rulers of his day and produced guidelines for the acquisition and maintenance of power by absolute rule.

What would you do with these items if you were told you had to keep and remember all of them?

Use the space provided to reflect on this thought experiment. What is the point of this experiment? What is the big idea or message of this thought experiment?

```


```

In the box above, our guess is that you made some reference or comment about knowing what to do with the first set of items, but not sure about what to do with the second set of items. Specifically, you have specific locations for placing eggs (the refrigerator), coat hangers (a closet), mulch (anywhere outside), a magazine (on a table), and soap (near a sink). In your mind, you likely thought of specific locations that made the acquisition, consolidation, and storage of those items relatively easy. So what happened with the second set of items?

For many of us, that list was unclear, overwhelming, and generated more questions than answers. Unless you are a social studies teacher, acquiring, consolidating, and storing those five items would prove to be quite difficult. The answer lies in our prior knowledge and how prior knowledge facilitates the acquisition, consolidation, and storage of new learning.

In the space below, generate your own explanation of how integrating prior knowledge supports learning. The opening thought experiment should help you generate your explanation.

```


```

We must explicitly teach our students to integrate their prior knowledge into new declarative, procedural, and conceptual learning.

The learning strategy in this module is **integrating prior knowledge into new learning.**

LEARNING INTENTION

We are learning about the role prior knowledge plays in new learning.

SUCCESS CRITERIA

I will know we have successfully completed this module when

- I can describe the benefits of learners activating their prior knowledge.

- I can explain how activating prior knowledge supports selective attention along with the other promising principles.

- I can map out a process for implementing time for learners to activate their prior knowledge in my classroom.

THE BENEFITS OF INTEGRATING PRIOR KNOWLEDGE

Integrating prior knowledge into new learning supports learners in attending to the most relevant content, skills, and understandings during a learning experience or task.

online resources

For more resources related to prior knowledge, visit the companion website at resources.corwin.com/howlearningworks.

This includes things they already know, things that they don't know yet, and things that they are not quite sure about in this new learning. When learners self-monitor, self-reflect, and self-evaluate how what they already know relates to what they are learning now, they are better at discerning what is relevant and irrelevant, and then hold that attention until a specific goal or outcome is accomplished.

Return to Module 6. We looked at three specific factors that influence our attention. List them here:

1.

2.

3.

Integrating prior knowledge into new learning supports learners as they make meaning of their new learning, while at the same time it retrieves previous learning. Make sure you circled *effective* for this strategy in Module 12. While integrating prior knowledge supports the selective attention of our learners, this strategy will also support the application of the other principles and practices as well.

Use the space provided to describe how you think integrating prior knowledge benefits motivation, attention, elaborate encoding, retrieval and practice, cognitive load, productive struggle, and feedback. You may need to flip back to earlier modules. "Retrieval and Practice" is done for you as an example.

For more resources related to how knowledge helps, visit the companion website at resources.corwin.com/howlearningworks.

INTEGRATING PRIOR KNOWLEDGE INTO NEW LEARNING

Motivation	
Attention	
Elaborate Encoding	
Retrieval and Practice	Retrieval and practice is the reconstructing of prior knowledge, skills, and understandings. When learners purposefully, intentionally, and deliberately integrate prior knowledge into new learning, they are engaging in retrieval and practice of that prior knowledge. Thus, this action is beneficial for both prior and new learning.
Cognitive Load	
Productive Struggle	
Feedback	

GETTING READY TO INTEGRATE PRIOR KNOWLEDGE

Let's try another experiment. Please read the following passage.

> The procedure is actually quite simple. First, you arrange things into different groups depending on their makeup. Of course, one pile may be sufficient depending on how much there is to do. If you have to go somewhere else due to lack of facilities, that is the next step; otherwise, you are pretty well set. It is important not to overdo any particular endeavor. That is, it is better to do too few things at once than too many. In the short run, this may not seem important, but complications from doing too many can easily arise. A mistake can be expensive as well. The manipulation of the appropriate mechanisms should be self-explanatory, and we need not dwell on it here. At first, the whole procedure will seem complicated. Soon, however, it will become just another facet of life. It is difficult to foresee any end to the necessity for this task in the immediate future, but then one never can tell. (Seidenberg & Farry-Thorn, 2020)

Return to the passage and circle, underline, or highlight what you think are the most important pieces of information from this passage. Much like the opening example of this module, the task of identifying the important information was difficult and likely lead to you simply picking things just to get through the task. But what if I told you that this passage was about doing the laundry? Now if you were to go back and circle, underline, and highlight the most important pieces of information, would this be different knowing that the passage is about doing laundry?

The context of the learning strongly influences the way we attend to the content.

Knowing the what, why, and how of the content sets the context of the learning. This context is communicated through learning intentions, success criteria, and relevant tasks and learning experiences. As part of the larger concept of teacher clarity, ensuring that our learners know the context of their learning is the first step in getting ready to integrate prior knowledge.

Use the space below to describe how you ensure your learners know the context of their learning. What specific strategies do you use to communicate or share the what, why, and how of learning?

online resources

For more resources related to the "Baseball Study" and clarity, visit the companion website at resources.corwin.com/ howlearningworks.

ENSURING THAT OUR LEARNERS KNOW THE CONTEXT OF THEIR LEARNING IS THE FIRST STEP IN GETTING READY TO INTEGRATE PRIOR KNOWLEDGE.

However, this is just the start. Simply throwing an objective on the board does not guarantee that learners will attend to that objective or integrate prior learning. This strategy must be explicitly taught, practiced, and supported in our classrooms.

A PROCESS FOR INTEGRATING PRIOR KNOWLEDGE

Let's look at a process for explicitly teaching this learning strategy to our students (see Figure 14.1).

 14.1 INTEGRATING PRIOR KNOWLEDGE

Create and share the what, why, and how of the learning (e.g., learning intentions and success criteria).	→	Learners engage in an analysis of the what, why, and how that identifies or retrieves prior knowledge.	→	The teacher and learners reflect on the specific needs of the learners before moving forward in the learning.

To move through this process, let's start with a specific example. Returning to the World History example at the beginning of this module, let's start with a set of learning intentions and success criteria from this classroom (see Figure 14.2).

online resources

For more resources related to memory, visit the companion website at resources.corwin.com/howlearningworks.

 14.2 EXAMPLES OF LEARNING INTENTIONS AND SUCCESS CRITERIA FOR A WORLD HISTORY CLASS

Topic: The Renaissance in Europe	
Learning Intentions	Today, we are learning about the economic effects of the Crusades so that we can understand the developments leading to the Renaissance.
Success Criteria	We know we are successful in our learning when • We can **describe** specific economic effects of the Crusades. • We can **explain** the relationship between the Church's rule and banking practices in Northern Italy. • We can **make inferences and support those inferences** about why the Renaissance could not have started elsewhere in Europe.

The first part of the process for explicitly teaching this learning strategy is creating and sharing the what, why, and how of the learning. However, this alone is not enough. We must scaffold learners' active engagement with the what, why, and how and then gradually remove that scaffold so that they self-regulate this process in their own learning.

The template on the next page provides a guided approach to direct learners toward the day's learning. A few examples are provided to get you started.

LEARNING INTENTIONS AND SUCCESS CRITERIA SELF-ASSESSMENT

What knowledge, skills, and understandings do you already have related to today's learning?

Concepts	I am very familiar with this concept.	I have heard of this concept before.	This is a new concept for me.
1. Example: Church's rule in Northern Italy			X
2.			
3.			
4.			
5.			
6.			

Skills	I am very familiar with this skill.	I have done this before.	This is a new skill for me.
1. Example: Making inferences	X		
2.			
3.			

Understanding	I am clear on this understanding.	I am aware of this understanding.	This is a new understanding for me.
1. Example: The Crusades had an economic impact that influenced the Renaissance.			X
2.			

In addition to learners identifying their level of familiarity or prior knowledge related to the content, skills, and understandings, it is important to provide opportunities for them to articulate what they are uncertain, unclear, or unaware of related to the new learning. This also offers us important data on where we should focus the learning experiences for this particular topic. For example, if learners indicate that they have no prior knowledge about the economic impact of the Crusades, we must then ensure that they have ample experiences and time to elaborately encode, engage in retrieval and practice, experience productive struggle, and receive feedback around this piece of content. Furthermore, we will have to monitor learners' cognitive load. Take a look at the template on the next page where learners can develop questions about the day's learning.

For more resources related to pre-questioning, visit the companion website at resources.corwin.com/howlearningworks.

SELF-ASSESSMENT REFLECTION

What specific words or phrases are unclear in today's learning intentions and success criteria?

Using your responses from above, develop a list of questions you have about today's learning.

List specific tasks you believe you will need to do to be successful in today's learning.

Take a moment and map out how you will explicitly teach learners to integrate prior knowledge into their new learning AND develop the capacity to self-assess where they do not have prior knowledge or experiences. An important aspect of using the gradual release of responsibility is to identify when you want learners to independently use this strategy. When do you want learners to self-monitor their own prior knowledge, self-reflect on what they do and don't know, and self-assess their current understanding? The space below provides an opportunity for you to plan for this release, as well as how and when learners will practice and get feedback on the use of this strategy.

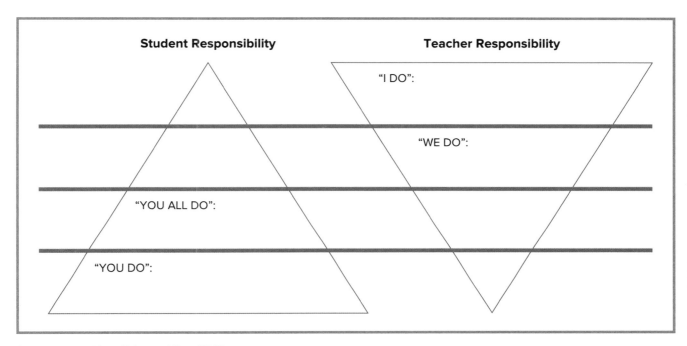

Source: Adapted from Fisher and Frey (2013).

✳ Annotated Reading

Not all learning starts with learning intentions and success criteria. For example, project-based experiences, performance-based tasks, or inquiry approaches to learning may come with a set of instructions, directions, or supporting materials. So, how do we build capacity in our learners to integrate prior knowledge into these tasks and thus attend to the most relevant content, skills, and understandings? There are additional strategies that students should learn that will contribute to the self-regulatory attributes that seem most desirable for learners: self-monitoring, self-evaluation, self-assessment, and self-teaching. Let's look at one of those now: annotated reading.

What Is Annotated Reading?

Annotated reading is an active reading strategy where learners "mark up" text based on what they believe is important or mark up areas that are unclear and create confusion for them. While you and your learners can co-create the "marks," some examples follow.

1. Circle keywords that you recognize and believe are important to the learning task or experience.

2. Underline key phrases that you believe are major ideas necessary for completing the learning task or experience.

3. Write a question mark next to anything confusing or unclear. Then formulate a question that you will ask the teacher or your peers.

4. Place an exclamation point next to information that helps you make a connection to something else. Write that "something else" in the margin.

The space below provides an opportunity for you to plan for the gradual release of annotated reading, as well as how and when learners will practice and get feedback on the use of this strategy.

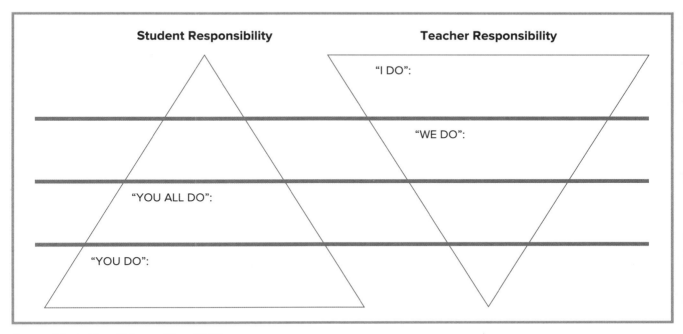

Source: Adapted from Fisher and Frey (2013).

Research has been very clear on the role of integrating prior knowledge into new learning. Furthermore, learners develop a tool kit of strategies that support their capacity for self-monitoring, self-reflecting, and self-assessing what they know and don't know about a particular topic. This, in the end, increases the probability that they are attending to the most relevant information during learning. In other words, they are not distracted by the number of times the ball is passed between those individuals wearing white shirts. They don't miss the giant gorilla walking across the room.

The explicit instruction of integration strategies ensures learning by design, not by chance.

For a video on attention and awareness, visit the companion website at resources.corwin.com/howlearningworks.

Checks for Understanding

Take a moment and return to the success criteria for this module. As you have done in the previous modules, respond to the following questions by "showing what you know." Attach student work samples, comments, or feedback to support your responses.

Know	Show (Generate a response to the question that "shows what you know"; include student work samples, comments, or feedback)
Can I describe the benefits of learners activating their prior knowledge?	
Can I explain how activating prior knowledge supports selective attention along with the other promising principles?	
Can I map out a process for implementing time for learners to activate their prior knowledge in my classroom?	

With strategies for upping motivation and attention in place, let's turn to the encoding of the most relevant information: summarizing.

LEARNING STRATEGY 3: SUMMARIZING

LEARNING INTENTION

We are learning about summarizing and how this strategy supports encoding.

SUCCESS CRITERIA

I will know we have successfully completed this module when

- I can describe what happens when learners summarize.

- I can explain how summarizing supports encoding along with the other promising principles.

- I can map out a process for implementing summarization strategies in my classroom.

Before we move forward in this playbook, take some time to review the experiences, tasks, and learning from the previous 14 modules. Then, summarize your learning in the box.

Summarizing requires that learners take information, identify the most important and relevant content, skills, or understandings, and then decide how different ideas are related to each other. Think back to the previous exercise asking you to summarize the previous 14 modules. Did you indeed take a large quantity of information, select what you felt was most important, and then blend the information together into a summary? Maybe you just created a list. Does that matter?

As it turns out, research on summarizing has addressed this very issue and will help us develop a definition of this particular learning strategy. Knowing what is meant by summarizing and what is not will help us explicitly teach our students an approach that moves their learning forward.

Below is a continuum of effectiveness. Place the following tasks on the line based on what you believe is their level of effectiveness in the acquisition, consolidation, and storage of learning after a person reads a 2,000-word nonfiction text.

1. After each page, write three lines of text that summarize the main point from that page.

2. While reading each page, take up to three lines of notes.

3. Write down, verbatim, three lines from each page deemed most important.

4. Copy all of the capitalized words in the text.

5. Do nothing—just read the 2,000-word nonfiction text.

Least Effective	Most Effective
●———————————————————————————————●	

online
resources

For more resources related to summarizing conditions and note-taking, visit the companion website at resources.corwin.com/howlearningworks.

Bretzing and Kulhavy (1979) conducted this exact study and found that the capitalized letter task was the least effective, and the summary and note-taking tasks were the most effective. So, your continuum should look like this:

		5		2	
Least Effective	4		3		1	Most Effective

If you return to your summary at the beginning of this module, which of these five conditions did you actually do for the exercise? Based on these results, what do you believe is required in summarizing for this particular strategy to be the most effective for learners?

The learning strategy in this module is **summarizing**.

LEARNING INTENTION

We are learning how summarizing influences student learning.

SUCCESS CRITERIA

I will know we have successfully completed this module when

- I can describe the essential characteristics of summarizing.

- I can explain how summarizing supports encoding along with the other promising principles.

- I can apply the gradual release of responsibility to explicitly teaching summarizing to my learners.

The work of Bretzing and Kulhavy (1979) is not the only work on summarizing. Research on this particular learning strategy is quite robust. Fiorella and Mayer (2015) reported on 30 experimental studies and John Hattie has identified three meta-analyses made up of 384 different studies. Together, these studies provide a clear definition of summarizing, as well as essential characteristics that provide the greatest benefit to the learner as they encode declarative, procedural, and conditional learning. Notice the word *encode* in the previous sentence. Summarizing helps with the encoding of learning, as well as retrieval and practice. For now, let's focus on encoding. Take a moment and return to Module 7. In that module, we looked at three specific factors associated with encoding. List them here:

1.

2.

3.

Summarizing enhances meaning making and scaffolds the discovery and application of patterns.

ESSENTIAL CHARACTERISTICS OF SUMMARIZING

Summarizing is effective when

1. The task involves identifying the most relevant content or main ideas of the lecture, text, a video clip, or a visual representation of a concept.

2. The task requires learners to create the summary using their own words—this relies heavily on their retrieval of prior knowledge and experiences.

3. The task requires learners to identify and articulate connections between the different content and ideas in the summary.

Effective summarizing requires the generative processing of declarative, procedural, and conditional knowledge. Furthermore, summarizing only moves learning forward if the summaries result in the relevant content and main ideas of the learning. The generated summaries, then, must be guided by the lea_____ int_____ and suc_____ cr_____a (see the previous module). If you filled in the missing letters for the terms *learning intentions* and *success criteria,* you are correct. This points out how this learning strategy supports other promising principles beyond elaborate encoding.

Use the space provided, as we have done in the previous two modules, to describe how summarizing benefits motivation, attention, elaborate encoding, retrieval and practice, cognitive load, productive struggle, and feedback. You may need to flip back to earlier modules. "Retrieval and practice" is done for you as an example.

SUMMARIZING

Motivation	
Attention	
Elaborate Encoding	

Retrieval and Practice	Summarizing learning requires learners to use their own words to generate summaries. Generating their own words to develop the summary requires that they retrieve those words, along with content, skills, and understandings from the learning experience or task. This is, by definition, retrieval and practice.
Cognitive Load	
Productive Struggle	
Feedback	

GETTING READY TO SUMMARIZE

To explicitly teach this strategy to our learners so that they can use this strategy in their own learning, we must first expand our perspective about how learners can summarize. We often view summarizing as the individual task of writing on an index card. This is a limited view and can limit the utility of this particular learning strategy. We can vary the way learners summarize, how they summarize, and with whom they summarize. Consider the following approaches to summarizing:

→ Learners can summarize individually or in a small group with their peers.

→ Learners can summarize by writing or talking.

→ Learners can develop a formal summary or informally summarize their learning.

Use the following chart to develop different strategies for summarizing in your own classroom. Notice that the chart encourages the use of technology to increase the number of opportunities for summarizing. Several parts of the chart contain examples to get you going.

online resources

For more resources related to summarizing in elementary school, visit the companion website at resources.corwin.com/howlearningworks.

DIFFERENT STRATEGIES FOR SUMMARIZING

	Examples	Potential Use of Technology
Individually	Learners develop on a notecard a "Tweet" or a 150-character summary about a video clip.	
Small Group		
Through Writing		
Through Talking		Learners submit a 90-second Flipgrid summarizing a concept.
Formal		
Informal		Learners submit a quick summary in a chat box.

A PROCESS FOR THE EXPLICIT INSTRUCTION OF SUMMARIZING

Before we move along any further in this module, let's make sure we are clear on the big ideas. For summarizing to be an effective learning strategy for our students, we must be sure we not only know the parameters of summarizing but are able to support learners as *they* learn the parameters of effective summarizing. Use the space provided and write down the big ideas associated with summarizing.

Summarizing is more than just writing down or verbally sharing a list of facts, thoughts, or ideas related to a particular topic. For summarizing to move learning forward, those facts, thoughts, and ideas MUST align with the what, why, and how of the learning experience or task. The process for explicitly teaching summarizing must start with ensuring learners are attending to the learning intentions and success criteria. You will notice the first step of this process is the second step of the process for integrating prior knowledge into new learning (see Figure 15.1).

15.1 SUMMARIZING PROCESS

Learners engage in an analysis of the what, why, and how that identifies and retrieves prior knowledge. ➡ Learners extract the key concepts, main ideas, and important details based on the what, why, and how of the learning experience or task. ➡ Learners develop a summary using their own words and connecting the key concepts, main ideas, and important details.

While all the previous modules have emphasized integrating the process into the gradual release of responsibility, this is particularly important with summarizing. Findings from many studies on summarizing emphasize that the quality of the summary matters and that the quality of the summary comes from the explicit instruction on summarizing in our classrooms. More than any other learning strategy in this playbook, we must teach this process to our students. Bean and Steenwyk (1984) found that explicitly teaching summarizing produced the greatest gains.

For the first part of this process, learners must take their self-assessment of the learning intentions and success criteria one step further and focus on the actions in the success criteria. Let's go back and look at the World History example from Module 14. You will notice something has changed about the chart (see Figure 15.2).

 15.2 **EXAMPLES OF LEARNING INTENTIONS AND SUCCESS CRITERIA FOR A WORLD HISTORY CLASS**

Topic: The Renaissance in Europe		
Learning Intentions	Today, we are learning about the economic effects of the Crusades so that we can understand the developments leading to the Renaissance.	
Success Criteria	We know we are successful in our learning when <ul><li>We can **describe** specific economic effects of the Crusades.</li><li>We can **explain** the relationship between the Church's rule and banking practices in Northern Italy.</li><li>We can **make inferences and support those inferences** about why the Renaissance could not have started elsewhere in Europe.</li></ul>	<ul><li>What are the economic effects of the Crusades?</li><li>What is the relationship between the Church's rule and banking practices in Northern Italy?</li><li>Why could the Renaissance not have started elsewhere?</li></ul>

When students revise the success criteria into questions that they can respond to, it helps them focus on the concepts, main ideas, and important details. From there, learners can answer each question individually before looking for patterns, trends, and connections across the success criteria. You have seen this modeled at the end of each module.

Then, one way to scaffold the extracting of concepts, main ideas, and important details is to have them highlight those patterns, trends, and connections. This is the second part of the process. Of course, through gradual release, this should be modeled, done collaboratively, and then independently done with practice and feedback.

LEARNING INTENTIONS AND SUCCESS CRITERIA SELF-ASSESSMENT AND MONITORING

Topic:		
Learning Intentions	Today, we are learning . . .	
Success Criteria	We know we are successful in our learning when	Guiding questions from success criteria:

The final part of this process is the development of the summary, which is drawn from the many strategies you developed on page 160 in this module. Keep in mind that summarization requires explicit instruction to ensure that quality summaries are generated. Make sure you circled *effective* for this strategy in Module 12 but make note that this strategy is susceptible to challenges unless we carefully map out a plan for integrating this into our students' learning.

Let's close this module by mapping out how you will explicitly teach learners to summarize. An important aspect of using the gradual release of responsibility is to identify when you want learners to independently summarize. The space below provides an opportunity for you to plan for this release, as well as how and when learners will practice and get feedback on the use of this strategy.

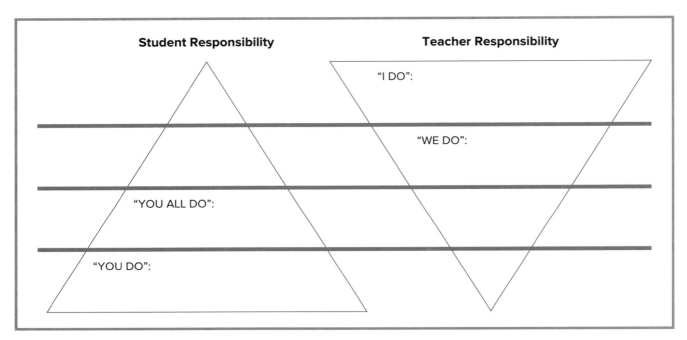

Source: Adapted from Fisher and Frey (2013).

Checks for Understanding

Take a moment and return to the success criteria for this module. As you have done in the previous modules, respond to the following questions by "showing what you know." Attach student work samples, comments, or feedback to support your responses.

Know	Show (Generate a response to the question that "shows what you know"; include student work samples, comments, or feedback)
Can I describe what happens when learners summarize?	
Can I explain how summarizing supports encoding along with the other promising principles?	
Can I map out a process for implementing summarization strategies in my classroom?	

16

LEARNING STRATEGY 4: MAPPING

In the previous module, we focused on the learning strategy of summarizing. To set up our next learning strategy, take a few moments and retrieve the essential characteristics of summarizing. We shared three in the last module; you can certainly add more in the space provided.

1.

2.

3.

Add some of your own.

4.

5.

We started this module by reviewing summarizing because mapping is a very similar learning strategy. Just as summarizing prompts learners to identify the key concepts, main ideas, and important details, mapping requires learners to do this as well. Mapping also prompts learners to explicitly identify connections among those key concepts, main ideas, and important details. Mapping, however, involves the creation of a spatial representation of those connections. This is where mapping and summarizing differ.

Learning by mapping occurs when learners are asked to convert a text lesson into a spatial arrangement of words, such as a concept map, knowledge map, or matrix graphic organizer. (Fiorella & Mayer, 2015, p. 38)

There were three specific types of mapping mentioned in the Fiorella and Mayer (2015) definition of mapping. List those three types here:

1.

2.

3.

online resources

For more resources related to mapping meta-analysis, visit the companion website at resources.corwin.com/howlearningworks.

These three specific types will be the focus of this module—mapping as a strategy for elaborate encoding, retrieval and practice, and, in some cases, productive struggle.

The learning strategy in this module is **mapping.**

LEARNING INTENTION

We are learning three different ways for learners to map out their learning.

SUCCESS CRITERIA

I will know we have successfully completed this module when

- I can compare and contrast the three different approaches to mapping.

- I can explain how mapping supports retrieval and practice, along with the other promising principles.

- I can apply the gradual release of responsibility to explicitly teach my students how to map.

THREE DIFFERENT WAYS TO MAP

Let's look at an example of each type of map and identify the similarities and differences between the three approaches. As you look at each example, use the Notes box to list your observations about each example. What do you notice? What do you wonder?

MATRIX GRAPHIC ORGANIZER PROVIDED TO LEARNERS

Name: _____

Story Summary

Character:

Book Title:

Author:

Problem:

Setting:

Theme:

Solution:

Image source: iStock/fjmoura

Notes

KNOWLEDGE MAPS CREATED BY A THIRD-GRADE LEARNER
AND A FIRST-GRADE LEARNER FROM ESSENTIAL VOCABULARY

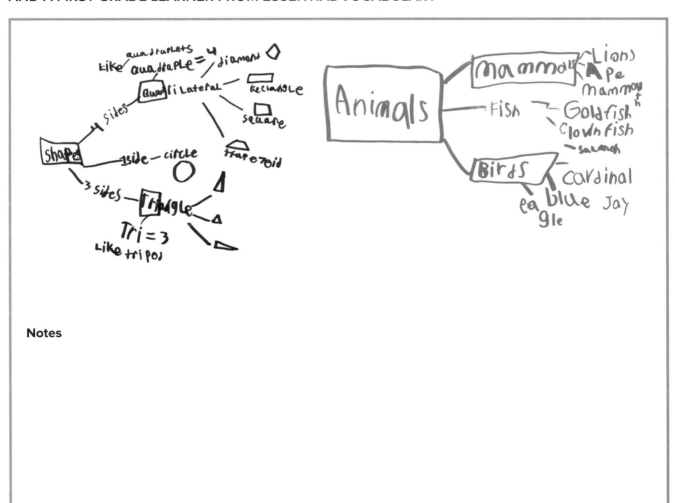

Notes

CONCEPT MAP GENERATED INDEPENDENTLY BY A LEARNER

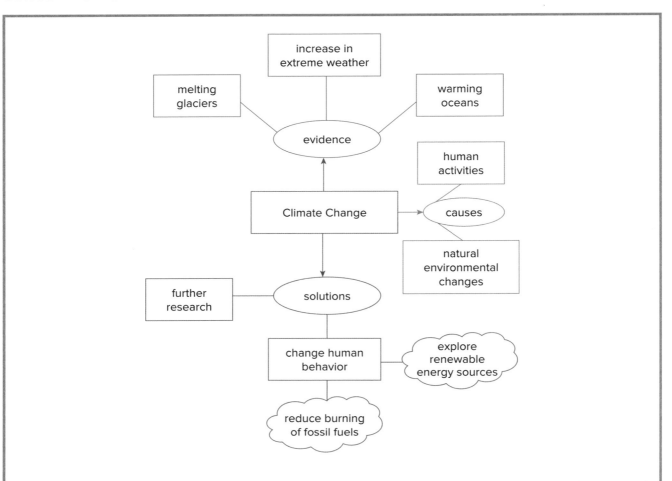

Source: Adapted from The Learning Center (n.d.). University of North Carolina, Chapel Hill. https://learningcenter.unc.edu/tips-and-tools/using-concept-maps. Creative Commons License.

Notes

Use the space provided to compile your notices and wonders and begin to compare and contrast the three approaches to mapping.

To talk about the similarities and differences between these three approaches to mapping, we first have to add some terminology or vocabulary. Mapping involves the spatial arrangement of nodes. Nodes are words—concepts, ideas, or details. Those nodes are linked together. These links are purposeful, intentional, and deliberate, not arbitrary connections. Return to the three examples on the previous pages.

For more resources related to knowledge maps, visit the companion website at resources.corwin.com/howlearningworks.

> Circle or highlight examples of nodes and links on each example.

For knowledge maps and concept maps, this was likely an easy request. The nodes and links are clear. For the graphic organizer, the nodes and links may be obvious simply because the graphic organizer has a predetermined structure based on the topic of the organizer. This predetermined structure also means that the learners have more constraints or limitations on how they map their learning. In a graphic organizer, learners simply fill in or complete the organizer with the requested information. In the example above, learners must recognize what the theme is and then write it into the graphic organizer.

Knowledge maps fall somewhere in between graphic organizers and concept maps. They have more constraints than a graphic organizer, fewer constraints than a concept map. For knowledge maps, learners must

1. Identify the most relevant content or ideas of the lecture, text, video clip, or visual representation of a concept.

2. Organize the content or ideas in a way that is meaningful to them.

3. Apply a predetermined set of links (e.g., can be, but if, means).

In a concept map, learners must

1. Identify the most relevant content or ideas of the lecture, text, video clip, or visual representation of a concept.

2. Organize the content or ideas in a way that is meaningful to them.

3. Explicitly identify and label the spatial connections between the different content and ideas in the concept map.

Take a moment and return once more to the three examples. Are you able to see the characteristics listed here in each of those examples? Then, using the continuum below, place each of the three types of maps somewhere on the continuum based on the level of constraints or limitations placed on the learner.

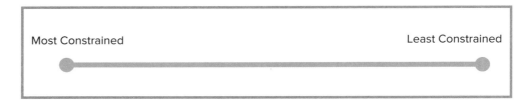

Most Constrained   Least Constrained

Mapping benefits motivation, attention, elaborate encoding, retrieval and practice, cognitive load, productive struggle, and feedback. As we have done in the previous two modules, use the space provided to describe how these promising principles and practices are integrated in mapping. You may need to flip back to earlier modules. "Cognitive Load" is done for you as an example.

MAPPING

Motivation	
Attention	
Elaborate Encoding	
Retrieval and Practice	

Cognitive Load	Generating the nodes and links in concept mapping and knowledge mapping is an example of germane cognitive load. Furthermore, organizing learning into a spatial representation or clusters, driven by connections, helps reduce extraneous cognitive load and monitor intrinsic cognitive load (e.g., taking complex material and organizing it into a spatial representation).
Productive Struggle	
Feedback	

GETTING READY FOR MAPPING

The central focus in teaching mapping to our learners is helping them to discern when to use a graphic organizer, knowledge map, or concept map. For the mapping strategy to be effective and move learning forward, learners must self-monitor, self-reflect, and self-evaluate as they spatially represent their learning; they also need to consider which approach to use to represent their learning. Here are some guiding questions to consider:

1. Is the learning about a standardized process or procedure (e.g., developing a narrative essay, the scientific method versus human impact on the environment)? In this situation, a graphic organizer may be more appropriate.

2. Are there clear delineations between various aspects or components of the topic (e.g., different types of polygons, different text features)? A graphic organizer may be best here as well.

3. Is the learning conditional (e.g., if-then relationships like the different types of triangles or rocks)? A knowledge map, with predetermined links, works well with conditional learning.

4. Are there multiple outcomes, variables, and interactions/relationships associated with the learning (e.g., climate change, Civil Rights Movement)? This level of complexity is often represented using a concept map.

THE CENTRAL FOCUS IN TEACHING MAPPING TO OUR LEARNERS IS HELPING THEM TO DISCERN WHEN TO USE A GRAPHIC ORGANIZER, KNOWLEDGE MAP, OR CONCEPT MAP.

The answers to each of these questions will provide insight into which approach to use and when. For now, use the chart below to brainstorm conditions associated with each approach. Refer to the previous guiding questions as needed. One is done for you as an example.

Approach to Mapping	When Is This Approach Most Appropriate?	Support for Learners (Strategy Instruction)
Graphic Organizer	1. Narrative essay—learners complete a graphic organizer as part of their pre-writing component. 2.	Learners will need support in matching specific components of the narrative essay with the graphic organizer and then the essay (e.g., what is each node and what goes where?).
Knowledge Map	1. 2.	
Concept Map	1. The relationship between human beings and climate change. 2.	Learners must be able to identify the concepts, skills, and ideas; and then arrange them in such a way that they can articulate the connections between concepts, skills, and understandings.

A PROCESS FOR THE EXPLICIT INSTRUCTION OF SUMMARIZING

Mapping is more than just writing down all the keywords and phrases and drawing a line between a few of these keywords and phrases. Mapping truly is a way for learners to spatially represent their learning and explicitly draw the connections and relationships among the learning. Once again, this process must start with ensuring learners are attending to the learning intentions and success criteria. This is becoming a reoccurring theme in this playbook. Learners must first start with their learning intentions and success criteria to ensure they are identifying relevant concepts, ideas, and details (see Figure 16.1).

16.1 **A PROCESS FOR THE EXPLICIT TEACHING OF MAPPING**

Learners extract the key concepts, ideas, and important details based on the what, why, and how of the learning experience or task.	→	Learners must arrange the concepts, ideas, and details into logical clusters. What goes with what?	→	Explicity articulate the connections or relationships using phrases or sentences.

The first part of this process relates to knowledge maps and concept maps. Learners must generate a list of concepts, skills, and understandings. Essentially learners are just developing a list of concepts, skills, and understandings from multiple sources (e.g., class notes, learning experiences and tasks, the textbook).

Pause for a moment and return to the examples of the knowledge map and concept map. You can see what concepts, skills, and understandings would have been on this learner's list. For the graphic organizer, learners are not developing lists from multiple sources. Instead, they are generating ideas to go into the predetermined structure (e.g., the theme, setting).

CONCEPTS, SKILLS, AND UNDERSTANDINGS

Topic:	
Concepts	1. 2. 3. 4. 5. 6.
Skills	1. 2. 3. 4. 5. 6.
Understandings	1. 2. 3. 4. 5. 6.

The second part of the process for explicitly teaching mapping to learners requires learners to take those concepts, ideas, and details and cluster them. What concepts can be grouped together? What ideas go together? What details are linked to each concept and idea? This sets up the drawing of the knowledge maps and concept maps. For the graphic organizer, this is where the learners decide what information goes into which part of the predetermined structure.

> Pause for a moment and return to the examples of the knowledge map and concept map. Notice how the learners that generated these two examples clustered their items (e.g., apple color, ripeness, as well as cellular respiration, light-dependent reactions). For the graphic organizer, learners are not developing lists from multiple sources. Instead, they are still generating ideas to go into the predetermined structure (e.g., the theme, setting).

For more resources related to multi-relational semantic maps, visit the companion website at resources.corwin.com/howlearningworks.

The final part of this process is the creation of the maps or the filling in of the graphic organizer. Just like summarizing, this strategy requires explicit instruction to ensure that the quality of the links and the quality of the information included in the graphic organizer are aligned with the learning intention and success criteria. Make sure you circled *effective* for this strategy in Module 12.

In the end, we want learners, without prompting, to decide that they want to generate a knowledge map after reading a section from their textbook. We want learners to take a week's worth of learning and generate a concept map that shows the relationships and interactions in the physiology of motion or ecosystems. But this takes time and explicit instruction. Learners will require both practice and feedback as they begin mapping their learning. The space below provides an opportunity for you to plan for this release, as well as how and when learners will practice and get feedback on the use of this strategy.

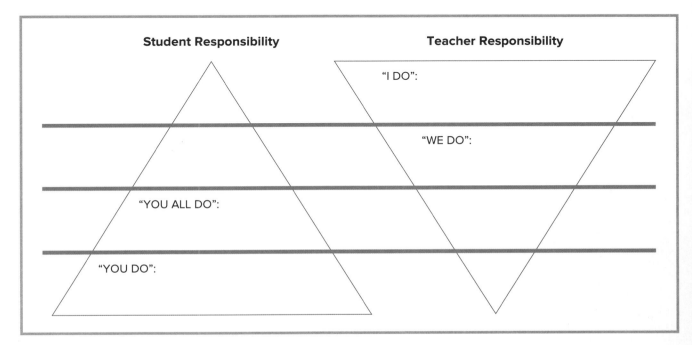

Source: Adapted from Fisher and Frey (2013).

Checks for Understanding

Take a moment and return to the success criteria for this module. As you have done in the previous modules, respond to the following questions by "showing what you know." Attach student work samples, comments, or feedback to support your responses.

Know	Show (Generate a response to the question that "shows what you know"; include student work samples, comments, or feedback)
Can I compare and contrast the three different approaches to mapping?	
Can I explain how mapping supports retrieval and practice, along with the other promising principles?	
Can I apply the gradual release of responsibility to explicitly teach my students how to map?	

17

LEARNING STRATEGY 5: SELF-TESTING

The term *testing* is one of the most disliked and, at the same time, underutilized concepts in education. If you mention the word *test* to your students or any group of students, there will be audible moans and groans. And that is only the distaste you can see and hear. There is likely internal anxiety moving through the classroom as well. Try this exercise with your own learners. Ask them what comes to mind when they hear the word *test*. How do their responses align with their responses to the Conceptions of Learning Survey in Module 1 on page 17?

Self-testing is a very efficient strategy that supports learners in self-monitoring, self-reflecting, and self-evaluating their learning. In 1909, Edwina Abbott conducted and published the very first study on self-testing.

Since then, there has been a large amount of research on the benefits of this learning strategy. However, we have to address a few misconceptions to ensure that when each of us uses the term *self-testing*, we are clear on the meaning of that term. As we move forward in this module, not only will we continue to focus on the gradual release of responsibility, but we will have to monitor the dispositions and attitudes of our learners toward this very efficient strategy.

online resources

For more resources related to the original study on the testing effect, visit the companion website at resources.corwin.com/howlearningworks.

The learning strategy in this module is **self-testing.**

LEARNING INTENTION	SUCCESS CRITERIA
We are learning about the role of self-testing in the acquisition, consolidation, and storage of learning.	I will know we have successfully completed this module when • I can describe what is meant by self-testing. • I can explain how self-testing benefits my learners. • I can apply the gradual release of responsibility to explicitly teaching students to engage in self-testing.

To get started, take a look at the following graph. You likely recognize that graph from Module 8 except this version is without any labels or descriptions. Without flipping back to that module, label, fill in, and add as many descriptors as you can, related to what this graph is and what information is conveyed through the graph.

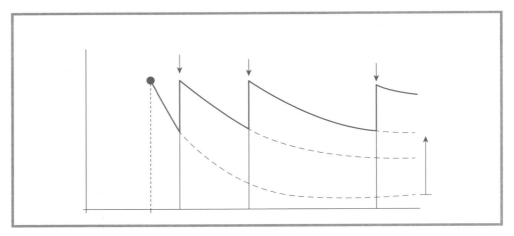

Now, if you would like to receive feedback on this task, flip back to page 80 in Module 8. How did you do? If you need to make revisions to your above responses, do so now.

Congratulations, you just participated in self-testing. Before we define what is meant by self-testing, look back at the previous paragraph and put a circle around the word *feedback*. We will come back to that later.

Self-testing occurs when learners respond to low-stakes practice questions about previously learned material. What separates self-testing, the highly effective learning strategy and focus of this module, from other forms of testing (i.e., standardized tests or unit tests) is that

1. Self-testing is low stakes or no stakes
2. Self-testing can be completed both within or outside of the learning task or experience
3. Self-testing is something learners engage in on their own

Using the Venn diagram below, compare and contrast self-testing with other forms of testing you use in your classroom. Be specific.

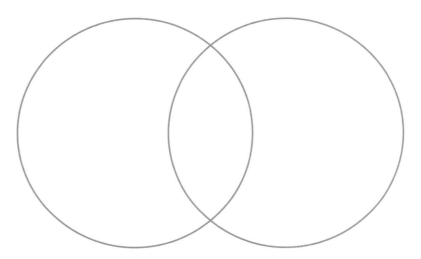

BENEFITS OF SELF-TESTING

Self-testing provides many benefits for learners. For example, when learners generate responses to low-stakes practice questions, they are engaging in the retrieval of declarative, procedural, and conditional learning. This benefit is enhanced when this practice testing is spaced out over time (e.g., spaced or distributed practice). Furthermore, when these low-stakes questions take on different forms (e.g., multiple-choice, free-response, or mixed variety), learners have the opportunity to access or retrieve their learning using different cues or prompts. For example, responding to a multiple-choice question requires a different kind of retrieval than a free-response question. However, in general, the benefits of self-testing are greater when learners must generate responses through free-response questions (Smith & Karpicke, 2014).

Using the space provided, generate a list of all the different ways learners can engage in self-testing. While they need to test themselves, rather than have us test them, this list will help us later on in the module when we embark on the gradual release of responsibility in self-testing. Many learners may simply have misconceptions about what is meant by self-testing.

For more resources related to different types of tests, visit the companion website at resources.corwin.com/howlearningworks.

Self-testing not only capitalizes on retrieval and practice, but when learners engage in practice testing, they also leverage the other promising principles and practices discussed in this playbook. Use the space provided to describe how self-testing benefits motivation, attention, elaborate encoding, retrieval and practice, cognitive load, productive struggle, and feedback. You may need to flip back to earlier modules. "Attention" is done for you as an example.

SELF-TESTING

Motivation	
Attention	If attention is the identifying, selecting, and focusing of our cognitive resources on specific learning, self-testing helps highlight what specifically needs to be focused on—especially when mistakes are made or learners get something wrong. It ups learners' awareness of what they need to work on in the next steps of their learning.
Elaborate Encoding	

(Continued)

(Continued)

Retrieval and Practice	
Cognitive Load	
Productive Struggle	
Feedback	

WHAT IF LEARNERS MAKE MISTAKES?

One of the concerns with self-testing is the possibility that the learner will get something wrong and won't be in our school or classroom so that we can address the mistake. Let's say that a seventh grader decides to engage in practice testing on the relationship between the circumference and area of a circle. In his or her attempt to answer conceptual, procedural, or application questions that they have selected from their textbook, the seventh grader makes several mistakes and gets many of the questions wrong. Is this a problem? The answer: It depends. Whether making a mistake is beneficial or harmful depends on the learners' access to corrective feedback.

When effective corrective feedback is provided, making mistakes and then correcting those errors based on the feedback enhances the benefits of self-testing. To make sure we support the giving and receiving of active feedback, flip back to Module 11 and list some of the characteristics of effective feedback. Use the space provided to create your list.

online
resources

For more resources related to the role of feedback, visit the companion website at resources.corwin.com/howlearningworks.

GETTING READY TO IMPLEMENT SELF-TESTING

To lay the foundation necessary to support learners in the implementation of this learning strategy, three specific areas must be addressed in our classroom.

1. We must motivate learners to engage in self-testing. After a while, we want them to be self-motivated to practice testing.

Returning to Module 5, how can you increase student interest, build their self-efficacy, establish effort-based attributions, and encourage deep motivation?

2.   We must increase their tools for self-questioning and support them in picking the right tool, at the right time, to get the maximum benefit from self-testing.

Returning to Module 8, specifically Figure 8.2, what tools would your learners benefit from as they engage in self-testing? Be specific. Those are the tools that we will implement through gradual release.

3.   We must plan for the giving and receiving of feedback, whether from us, from their peers, or through online platforms (e.g., IXL, Reflex Map, Achieve3000).

Feedback varies in terms of timing, amount, mode, and audience. Return to Module 11 and describe how you will vary feedback to enhance the effects of self-testing.

A PROCESS FOR IMPLEMENTING SELF-TESTING

Let's be very honest: getting learners to practice is challenging. Self-testing is no exception. There are challenges to all the learning strategies we have discussed in this playbook. That is expected and is a normal part of teaching and learning. For example, goal setting takes time and careful monitoring. Integrating prior knowledge involves learners realistically self-assessing their familiarity with content, skills, and understandings. Without explicitly teaching summarizing, learners may struggle and mapping requires selecting the right approach to mapping. Again, this is expected and normal. When it comes to practice through self-testing, the challenge lies in simply getting learners to do it. However, what appears to be a potentially powerful approach is to integrate other learning strategies into this process. Let's look at the process to uncover what we mean (see Figure 17.1).

17.1 A PROCESS FOR THE EXPLICIT TEACHING OF SELF-TESTING

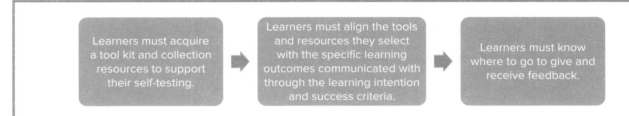

The first part of this process was initiated on page 181 of this module. You generated a list of tools that would benefit your learners as they engage in self-testing, and these tools must then be explicitly taught to learners. Again, we are moving away from simply using evidence-based practices "on" our learners to explicitly teaching them learning strategies that they can use on their own. We do this by

➡ Modeling the specific strategy within the context of self-testing

➡ Making learning visible so that learners can attribute the self-testing to their growth

➡ Modeling what to do when they don't know what to do, so they can do this when we are not there to immediately help them

➡ Modeling and practicing the giving and receiving of feedback

The second part of this process is helping learners align tools and resources available to them with the learning intention and success criteria.

> The learning intention informs us *what* to practice test. The success criteria tell us *how* to practice test.

Take, for example, the following success criteria:

➡ I can model data using an equation.

➡ I can explain the human impact on an ecosystem.

➡ I can identify key details of my reading and explain how they support the main idea.

➡ I can analyze my work to identify areas where I need additional practice.

Take a moment and circle the verbs in each of the above criteria. The verbs *model, explain, identify,* and *analyze* tell us and our learners how they are to practice. In other words, how is a learner supposed to practice with data and equations? By modeling.

How is a learner supposed to practice with human impact on an ecosystem? By explaining. The verb not only tells us and our learners how to practice but also narrows down our choice of tools. The generative processes of the tool should *match* the generative processes implied by the verb. In the space below, re-write the previous sentence. That statement is really important.

The generative processes . . .

If the verb in the success criteria is *describe,* the tools we select and the ones we want our learners to select should give them practice describing. In the chart below, use your responses to item 2 on page 184 of this module as a starting point to generate tools that align to the verbs in example success criteria. One is done for you as an example.

Success Criteria	Verb	Examples of Aligned Tools and Resources
I can **model** data using an equation.	Model	
I can **explain** the human impact on an ecosystem.	Explain	Use Flipgrid to verbally practice explaining this impact.
I can **identify** key details of my reading and explain how they support the main idea.	Identify	
I can **analyze** my work to identify areas where I need additional practice.	Analyze	

SELF-TESTING TOOLS

Success Criteria	Verb	Examples of Aligned Tools and Resources

The final part of this process involves the feedback. As we have done in each of the previous models, this requires us to model where to get the feedback and what to do with that feedback once we have it (e.g., anchor charts, one-on-one conferencing, exemplars, rubrics, teacher modeling). The key to this component is to maintain low stakes. Feedback is not a grade. The second we provide a grade, self-testing moves from low stakes to high stakes and the motivation to use this as a learning strategy moves to simply getting a grade.

In the end, we want learners, without prompting, to practice. Whether through goal setting, self-assessing, or utilizing one of the other learning strategies presented in this playbook, we want our learners to self-regulate both the strategy of self-testing and when to use practice testing to enhance their learning.

Before we map out the gradual release of responsibility for self-testing, let's add in some bonus material.

online resources

For more resources related to scheduling self-testing and reciprocal teaching, visit the companion website at resources.corwin.com/howlearningworks.

BONUS MATERIAL!

✳ Cooperative Learning

One approach for supporting independent self-testing is using cooperative learning as part of the scaffolding toward self-testing. Cooperative learning is defined as

> A pedagogical strategy through which two or more learners collaborate to achieve a common goal. Typically, cooperative learning seeks to foster positive interdependence through face-to-face interactions, to hold individual group members accountable for the collective project, and to develop interpersonal skills among learners. Cooperative learning aims to enable learners to engage in more complex subject matter than students would typically be able to master. (Visible Learning Meta[X], 2021)

Simply using cooperative learning does not necessarily lead to self-testing. However, we can build learners' self-efficacy and effort attribution by assigning roles within cooperative learning tasks that involve self-testing. For example, learners might be placed in a cooperative learning experience where one of the rotating roles is the *Inquisitor*. This individual would be responsible for generating questions around the particular task. The gradual release aspect of this approach and role would be as follows:

1. Initially provide pre-created questions that they can select and use in the cooperative learning task.

2. Then, provide question stems and the *Inquisitor* must finish the second half of the questions.

3. And then, question starters require the *Inquisitor* to write a larger part of the questions.

4. Finally, the *Inquisitor* generates his or her own questions.

Another specific strategy that supports self-questioning is the use of reciprocal teaching.

Much like assigning roles in cooperative learning, reciprocal teaching offers every learner the opportunity to generate questions and responses around a text-based task.

The space below provides an opportunity for you to plan for this release, as well as how and when learners will practice and get feedback on the use of this strategy.

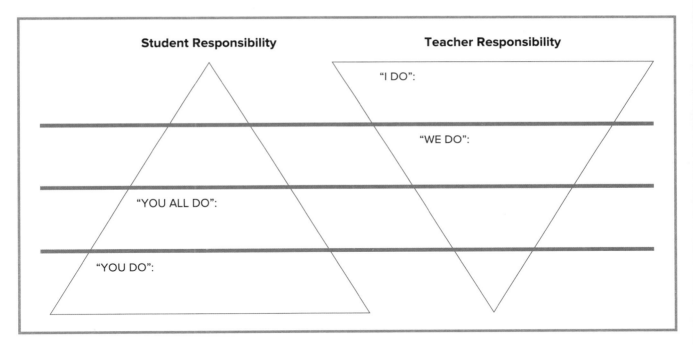

Source: Adapted from Fisher and Frey (2013).

>>> Checks for Understanding

Take a moment and return to the success criteria for this module. As you have done in the previous modules, respond to the following questions by "showing what you know." Attach student work samples, comments, or feedback to support your responses.

Know	Show (Generate a response to the question that "shows what you know"; include student work samples, comments, or feedback)
Can I describe what is meant by self-testing?	
Can I explain how self-testing benefits my learners?	
Can I apply the gradual release of responsibility to explicitly teaching students to engage in self-testing?	

LEARNING STRATEGY 6: ELABORATIVE INTERROGATION

We have come a long way since the start of this playbook. As we enter into this next module, it might be time to pause and review the previous five learning strategies. The chart below lists those strategies and then provides a space for you to reflect on the "why" behind those strategies. Take a moment and complete the chart; provide as much detail as possible and examples from your own classroom.

Learning Strategy	Why Does This Particular Strategy Have the Potential to Accelerate Student Learning?
Goal Setting	

(Continued)

(Continued)

Learning Strategy	Why Does This Particular Strategy Have the Potential to Accelerate Student Learning?
Integrating Prior Knowledge	
Summarizing	
Mapping	
Self-Testing	

Whether you realized this at the time, you just participated in elaborative interrogation. Elaborative interrogation is defined as a questioning technique that calls for readers to generate an explanation for an explicitly stated fact by asking questions such as

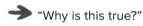 "Why is this true?"

 "Why does this make sense?"

Or simply,

➡ "Why?"

Unlike more typical textbook questions, which ask "what" instead of "why," elaborative interrogation has been shown to promote learning with text-based experiences or tasks (Visible Learning Meta[X], 2021).

The learning strategy in this module is **elaborative interrogation.**

LEARNING INTENTION

We are learning about elaborative interrogation.

SUCCESS CRITERIA

I will know we have successfully completed this module when

- I can describe what is meant by elaborative interrogation.

- I can describe different ways to encourage elaborative interrogation.

- I can apply the gradual release of responsibility to explicitly teaching students to engage in elaborative interrogation on their own.

BENEFITS OF ELABORATIVE INTERROGATION

Starting with the seminal work of Pressley et al. (1987), elaborative interrogation has been thoroughly investigated across many different groups of learners (e.g., age, disability status) and many different types of learning (e.g., declarative, procedural, and conditional).

However, the findings of the research suggest that elaborative interrogation is more effective with factual material. The chart on the next page contains factual statements from various content areas and grade levels. In the column on the right, create an elaborative interrogation question.

online resources

For more resources related to elaborative interrogation, visit the companion website at resources.corwin.com/howlearningworks.

For more resources related to the elaborate encoding effect size study, visit the companion website at resources.corwin.com/howlearningworks.

Examples of Elaborative Interrogation Questions

1. "Why is this true?"

2. "Why does this make sense?"

3. "Why?"

4. "Why would this be true of _____ and not _____?"

There are several examples in the chart to get you going.

Factual Statement	Potential Elaborative Interrogation
High School Trigonometry: Trigonometric functions are not invertible, because they are periodic. Domain restrictions on trigonometric functions are necessary in order to determine the inverse trigonometric function.	Why are trigonometric functions not invertible?
Middle School World Geography: The physical features of Latin America and the Caribbean have influenced their settlement and development.	
Fifth-Grade Science: Sometimes when two or more substances are combined, they do not lose their identifying characteristics.	Why would this be true of some substances and not others?
Second-Grade Reading: Illustrations and images contribute to and clarify text.	

Elaborative interrogation draws on multiple principles from the science of learning. Although retrieval and practice and productive struggle are obvious connections, simply asking "Why?"—"Why does it make sense that . . . ?" or "Why is this true?"—not only capitalizes on retrieval and practice and productive struggle but leverages other promising principles and practices as well. Use the space provided to describe how elaborative interrogation benefits motivation, attention, elaborate encoding, retrieval and practice, cognitive load, productive struggle, and feedback. Flip back through the other modules if necessary. "Motivation" is done for you.

ELABORATIVE INTERROGATION

Motivation	Asking learners "why" often taps into their own interests about a particular topic. Elaborative interrogation around something that interests them will increase their motivation. Even if learners are not immediately interested in a topic, going below the surface to uncover the why behind the learning will increase motivation through enhancing their sense of agency.
Attention	
Elaborate Encoding	
Retrieval and Practice	
Cognitive Load	
Productive Struggle	
Feedback	

Let's return to the idea of productive struggle. As you might have noticed from the two previous tasks, elaborative interrogation can easily disrupt the "Goldilocks Zone" of productive struggle. Flip back to Module 10. What are some challenges that we may face in implementing elaborative interrogation? List a few of them here.

GETTING READY TO IMPLEMENT ELABORATIVE INTERROGATION

Recognizing the challenges you described in the previous exercise provides a greater chance that we can support our learners in developing the capacity for and ultimately using elaborative interrogation independently. Several prerequisite skills will enhance the implementation of this learning strategy.

1. We must ensure learners have access to the necessary resources for "finding things out." For example, if learners do not immediately know why trigonometric functions are not invertible, do they have the resources for finding the answer?

How will you not only ensure the necessary resources are available, but how will you incorporate this into your plan for the gradual release of responsibility?

2. We must explicitly teach our learners the different types of questions by first using examples and non-examples, then question frames, on to question stems, and then finally the opportunity to develop their own questions of "why."

Use this space to research and describe different types of questions (e.g., open versus closed, divergent versus convergent). How will you ensure learners have the capacity and confidence to ask questions of both you, their peers, and then themselves?

BONUS MATERIAL!

 **Jigsaw**

Elaborative interrogation is also effective in small group settings. Similar to the cooperative learning implementation of self-testing, we can create a learning experience that allows learners to practice elaborative interrogation within our classrooms. This makes us available to provide feedback and other scaffolds as they develop the capacity and dispositional skills to ask "why is this true?"; "why does this make sense?"; or even simply "why?"

A jigsaw is one specific strategy for structuring this work.

For more resources related to the jigsaw classroom, visit the companion website at resources.corwin.com/howlearningworks.

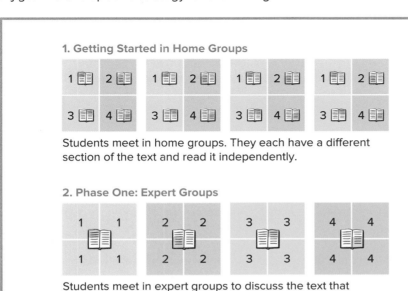

1. Getting Started in Home Groups

Students meet in home groups. They each have a different section of the text and read it independently.

2. Phase One: Expert Groups

Students meet in expert groups to discuss the text that they have in common.

(Continued)

(Continued)

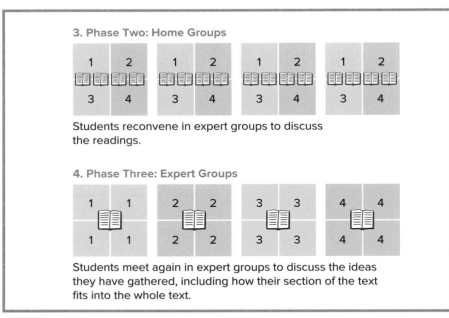

3. Phase Two: Home Groups

Students reconvene in expert groups to discuss the readings.

4. Phase Three: Expert Groups

Students meet again in expert groups to discuss the ideas they have gathered, including how their section of the text fits into the whole text.

Source: Adapted from Fisher and Frey (2018).

Learners are assigned to an expert group in which they develop expertise in a particular idea, concept, or topic. Each learner understands that he or she will be responsible for teaching his or her classmates the declarative, procedural, or conditional knowledge he or she has gained in their expert group when they return to their home group. For example, the teacher might develop expert groups on each application of the derivative (i.e., related rates, mean value, critical points, graphing, maximization and minimization problems, and differential equations). In science, an expert group could be developed for each type of map (i.e., bathymetric, geologic, topographic, weather, and star chart). What about learners exploring different genres of writing? In a World Geography course, expert groups might focus on different aspects of a country's geography (e.g., physical, cultural, human geography). Not to belabor the point, but this would work in physical education. For example, middle school learners could jigsaw different exercises for raising heart rate.

After an allotted amount of time, learners return to their home groups and teach the material to the other members. At the end of the teaching, learners return to their expert groups one final time to reflect on their experiences. Self-explanation and self-teaching are woven throughout the jigsaw strategy.

Before moving on, respond to the reflective question on the next page.

How does the jigsaw strategy support learners building their capacity for elaborative interrogation?

A PROCESS FOR IMPLEMENTING ELABORATIVE INTERROGATION

18.1 A PROCESS FOR THE EXPLICIT TEACHING OF ELABORATIVE INTERROGATION

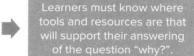

Learners must develop the expectation that they will have to answer the "why" in the classroom. → Learners must know where tools and resources are that will support their answering of the question "why?". → Learners must know where to go to give and receive feedback.

We set the tone for elaborative interrogation every time a learner gives a response to a question (see Figure 18.1). If a learner responds "The answer is 2," whether or not they are prepared to explain why the answer is 2 depends on the tone we set prior to this exchange. The first part of this process starts on day one in our classroom. For example, a teacher we know has a sign in the back of her classroom with the letters W – M – Y – S – T. Large enough to see from across the school, those letters stand for "What Makes You Say That?" As the year progresses, all she has to do is point to the poster after a learner has responded to a question, and they immediately begin to justify their response with evidence from the learning experience or task.

The second part of this process is helping learners identify tools and resources available to them when they do not know. Return to the factual statements and questions you generated on page 194 of this module. What tools would support a learner in "finding out" why, rather than waiting on someone to tell them the answer? For example, let's look at the fifth-grade science example: why would this be true of some substances and not others? Does your classroom have a science center? Could the learner look up the answer using their laptop computer? Is there a literacy center that contains books on mixtures and solutions?

If we are going to use elaborative interrogation, we must create a learning environment that supports this learning strategy. If students are not going to be allowed to get out of their seats, visit the media center, or step away from the current learning experience or task to find an answer, why implement this learning strategy? Use the space below to describe what guidelines or parameters you will need to create an environment conducive for elaborative interrogation.

SELF-TESTING TOOLS

Factual Statements	Potential Elaborative Interrogation	Examples of Tools and Resources

LIKE SELF-TESTING, ELABORATIVE INTERROGATION RELIES ON EFFECTIVE FEEDBACK.

Like self-testing, elaborative interrogation relies on effective feedback. As we have done in each of the previous models, this requires us to model where to get the feedback and what to do with that feedback once we have it. Some questions to consider include

1. How will learners share their answers to the questions "Why is this true?"; "Why does this make sense?"; or even simply "Why?" Will they simply self-explain or self-teach?

2. How will they get feedback on their responses to ensure we do not perpetuate misconceptions?

3. How will we provide feedback, but not in a way that discourages future elaborative interrogation?

The key to this component and self-testing is to maintain low stakes. This learning strategy is not for a grade either.

In the end, we want learners to naturally ask *Why*? We want them to know more than just declarative, procedural, and conditional knowledge from our classrooms. Instead of reading or hearing about earthworms, we want them to ask why they surface in a rainstorm. Why did F. Scott Fitzgerald write *The Great Gatsby?* Why is the slope of a vertical line undefined and not infinite? Whether through goal setting, self-assessing, or utilizing one of the other learning strategies presented in this playbook, we want our learners to use this powerful approach to move beyond surface-level understanding. We want them to be scuba divers, not snorkelers. And, as it turns out, this is a very effective learning strategy.

And for one final time in this playbook, use the space below to plan for this release, as well as how and when learners will practice and get feedback on the use of this strategy.

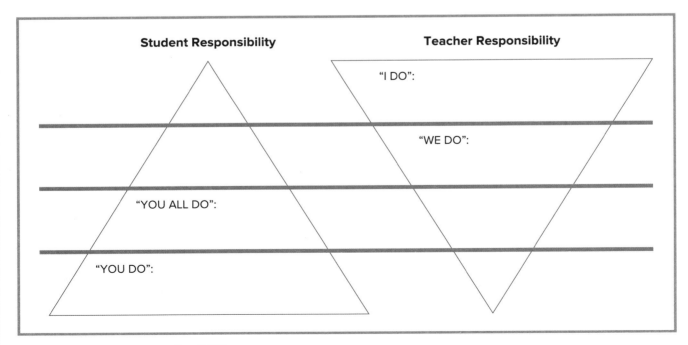

Source: Adapted from Fisher and Frey (2013).

>>> Checks for Understanding

Take a moment and return to the success criteria for this module. As you have done in the previous modules, respond to the following questions by "showing what you know." Attach student work samples, comments, or feedback to support your responses.

Know	Show (Generate a response to the question that "shows what you know"; include student work samples, comments, or feedback)
Can I describe what is meant by elaborative interrogation?	
Can I describe different ways to encourage elaborative interrogation?	
Can I apply the gradual release of responsibility to explicitly teaching students to engage in elaborative interrogation on their own?	

PART

IV

In this section:

Module 19. Generating and Gathering Evidence

19

GENERATING AND GATHERING EVIDENCE

From the very start of our journey through this playbook, we established two major ideas about how learning works and implementing promising principles or practices into our classroom:

1. The science of learning offers promising principles or practices that *may* work in our classrooms. However, we must make *adaptations* to these principles or practices that reflect the *local context of the classroom* and then *generate evidence* that allows both us and our learners to determine if learning has occurred.

2. The science of learning offers learning strategies that we should explicitly teach to our students to build their capacity and efficacy in their own independent learning journey. We want our students to take ownership of their learning and know what to do to move their learning forward when we are no longer their teacher.

Please return to the introduction of this playbook and list the four characteristics we want our learners to develop through the explicit instruction of learning strategies:

1.

2.

3.

4.

As we strive to achieve the two main ideas, we must engage in a process for evaluating whether a specific finding from the science of learning and learning strategies is having an impact on our learners. This final module walks through our role as evaluators of impact.

PLANNING FOR EVALUATION

To be evaluators of our impact, we must plan for evaluation. This includes

➡ Having and sharing clarity about learning

➡ A plan for gathering evidence

➡ A plan for collecting and organizing evidence

➡ A plan for making sense of the evidence

> **TO BE EVALUATORS OF OUR IMPACT, WE MUST PLAN FOR EVALUATION.**

Having and sharing clarity around learning involves three reflective questions (see Figure 19.1):

➡ Where we are going?

➡ How is it going?

➡ Where will we go next?

19.1 THREE QUESTIONS FOR PLANNING EVALUATION

Where are we going?	This component of the evaluation process looks at the intended learning target and the criteria for success. This can include content, as well as specific skills and understandings. **Example:** Students may be learning about watersheds, the War of 1812, or exponential growth at the same time they are developing their skills in summarizing.
How is it going?	This component draws from evidence generated by the learners to establish where they are making progress and where additional learning is needed. Similar to the first question, this includes content, skills, and understandings. **Example:** Evidence suggests learners are making progress in identifying the author's purpose, but when working with their "shoulder buddy" their summaries are simply repeating all the details.
Where will we go next?	This final component makes meaning of the generated evidence and uses that meaning making to plan the next steps in teaching and learning. **Example:** To better clarify what is meant by summarizing, the teacher plans to engage learners in co-constructing success criteria for "what makes a good summary." This involves comparing and contrasting examples and non-examples.

Looking specifically at the first question, where are we going, this requires us to leverage the learning intentions and success criteria associated with the learning experience or task. We have mentioned these two components of our classroom several times throughout the playbook. Their importance cannot be overstated. If we—both we and our students—are not clear on what they are learning, why they are learning it, and what success looks like, we can hardly identify promising principles and learning strategies to support the journey.

SUCCESS CRITERIA AND EVALUATION

Success criteria articulate what evidence learners must produce, what they must say and do, to demonstrate their progress toward the learning intention. In addition to success criteria providing guardrails for aligning our choice of strategies and supporting more goal-directed behavior in our learners, success criteria help us to be better evaluators of our impact.

Use the space provided to describe how success criteria support the promising principles or practices and the learning strategies in this playbook. Be sure to include specific examples from your classroom. We have provided examples to get you started.

Promising Principle or Practice	How Is This Supported by Success Criteria?	Examples From My Classroom
Motivation		
Attention	The success criteria help learners know what to look for or direct their attention to during the learning experience or task. If the success criteria are about identifying and describing the parts of a cell, learners are tipped off in what they need to attend to in the learning.	
Elaborate Encoding		

Promising Principle or Practice	How Is This Supported by Success Criteria?	Examples From My Classroom
Retrieval and Practice		
Cognitive Load		The success criteria are clear, specific, and concise to avoid cognitive overload.
Productive Struggle		
Feedback	The feedback provided is specifically aligned with the success criteria.	
Goal Setting		
Integrating Prior Knowledge		Once I share the success criteria with my learners, I ask them to list the prior learning that is needed to be successful. Then they work with a partner to make sure they are comfortable with those prior concepts or ideas.

(Continued)

(Continued)

Promising Principle or Practice	How Is This Supported by Success Criteria?	Examples From My Classroom
Summarizing		
Mapping		
Self-Testing		
Elaborative Interrogation		

PLANNING TO GATHER EVIDENCE

When planning to evaluate impact, formative assessments or checks for understanding provide opportunities to generate evidence that we can gather and evaluate. As we move forward in learning, we must partner with our learners to actively and continuously monitor student learning. These checks for understanding can range in complexity, intensity, and the means by which learners make their thinking visible. For example, checks for understanding can be written, verbal, or kinesthetic, depending on the criteria for success. The more directly and quickly we can obtain the necessary evidence, the better. Using success criteria from Module 14, let's look at an example in Figure 19.2.

19.2 EXAMPLE OF AN EVIDENCE-GATHERING PLAN

Criteria for Success	Tasks for Gathering Evidence
We can **describe** specific economic effects of the Crusades.	Learners will be asked to describe these effects to a neighbor; engage in a **three-minute write** midway through class; and complete an exit ticket at the end of class.
We can **explain** the relationship between the Church's rule and banking practices in Northern Italy.	Various activities include **think-pair-share using guiding questions**; **student questioning during direct instruction**; guided practice with examples from the textbook; and an exit ticket using clickers.
We can **make inferences and support those inferences** about why the Renaissance could not have started elsewhere in Europe.	Various activities include looking at contrasting cases during direct instruction to identify essential characteristics of the Renaissance; independently sorting different conditions and then writing out reasons for sorting categories; creating a **jigsaw** to identify the essential characteristics of the region; and **developing a concept map**.

Source: Adapted from Sweeney and Harris (2016).

Notice that the verbs in the success criteria are highlighted, along with specific tasks for gathering the evidence. The highlighted tasks are listed here. Next to each task, identify which promising principle or learning strategy they use. There may be more than one answer.

Three-minute write:

Think-pair-share using guiding questions:

Student questioning during direct instruction:

Jigsaw:

Developing a concept map:

EXAMPLE OF AN EVIDENCE-GATHERING PLAN

Criteria for Success	Tasks for Gathering Evidence

Source: Adapted from Sweeney and Harris (2016).

PLANNING TO COLLECT AND ORGANIZE EVIDENCE

In addition to planning the evidence to gather, we have to develop ways of collecting or organizing the evidence about declarative, procedural, and conditional learning. However, what is new in this playbook is the collecting of evidence about students' use of learning strategies and the impact of that use on their learning growth. Collecting an entrance ticket, exit ticket, or other student-generated artifacts is one way of obtaining the evidence. In addition, there needs to be a way of organizing evidence so that we can make meaning of student responses. Rich conversations, interactions, and actions that occur outside of tangible artifacts collected can also be used to determine impact (see Figure 19.3).

19.3   SAMPLE RECORD-KEEPING SHEET FOR COLLECTING EVIDENCE

Criteria for Success	Observed Doing	Heard Saying	Saw Writing
We can **describe** specific economic effects of the Crusades.			
We can **explain** the relationship between the Church's rule and banking practices in Northern Italy.			
We can **make inferences and support those inferences** about why the Renaissance could not have started elsewhere in Europe.			
Learning Strategies	**Observed Doing**	**Heard Saying**	**Saw Writing**
Summarizing			
Self-Testing			
Elaborative Interrogation			
Mapping			

Source: Adapted from Sweeney and Harris (2016).

RECORD-KEEPING SHEET FOR COLLECTING EVIDENCE

Criteria for Success	Observed Doing	Heard Saying	Saw Writing

Learning Strategies	Observed Doing	Heard Saying	Saw Writing
Summarizing			
Self-Testing			
Elaborative Interrogation			
Mapping			

Source: Adapted from Sweeney and Harris (2016).

When we gather evidence through seeing and listening, we gain insight into learners' understanding, dispositions, and motivations. Collecting evidence through a handout limits our evaluation to whether or not they completed the handout, nothing more.

MAKING SENSE OF THE EVIDENCE

Evaluating and organizing the evidence guides us in making decisions about *what happens next* in our teaching and their learning. We evaluate evidence by noticing the actions of our learners that reflect their understanding of the content and skills, as well as their implementation and use of specific learning strategies. We must critically reflect on the gradual release of responsibility.

➡ What do I do next?

➡ What do we do next?

➡ What do learners collaboratively need to do next?

➡ What do learners independently need to do next?

CONCLUSION

In the end, we must be fully aware of the impact resulting from the decisions we have made in our classrooms. From adapting promising principles or practices based on the local context of our classrooms, to explicitly teaching strategies to our learners, if what we are doing moves learning forward, we must keep doing it. But as we continue to do what works best, we must create a learning environment that releases the responsibility to our learners. When the semester ends or the year is over, will our learners know what to do when they don't know what to do, and we are not around? That is how learning is *supposed* to work.

WHEN WE GATHER EVIDENCE THROUGH SEEING AND LISTENING, WE GAIN INSIGHT INTO LEARNERS' UNDERSTANDING, DISPOSITIONS, AND MOTIVATIONS.

References

Abbott, E. E. (1909). On the analysis of the factors of recall in the learning process. *Psychological Monographs, 11*, 159–177.

Almarode, J., Fisher, D., Thunder, K., & Frey, N. (2021). *The success criteria playbook. A hands-on guide to making learning visible and measurable*. Corwin.

Bean, T. W., & Steenwyk, F. L. (1984). The effect of three forms of summarization instruction on sixth graders' summary writing and comprehension. *Journal of Reading Behavior, 16*(4), 297–306.

Bjork, R. A. (1975). *Retrieval as a memory modifier: An interpretation of negative recency and related phenomena*. In Information processing and cognition: The Loyola Symposium.

Blackburn, B. R. (2018). *Rigor is not a four-letter word*. Routledge.

Bretzing, B. H., & Kulhavy, R. W. (1979). Notetaking and depth of processing. *Contemporary Educational Psychology, 4*(2), 145–153.

Brookhart, S. M. (2008). How to give effective feedback to your students. ASCD.

Chew, S. L., & Cerbin, W. J. (2020). The cognitive challenges of effective teaching. *Journal of Economic Education, 52*(1), 17–40.

Dekker, S., Lee, N. C., Howard-Jones, P., & Jolles, J. (2012). Neuromyths in education: Prevalence and predictors of misconceptions among teachers. *Frontiers in Psychology, 3*(429), 1–8.

Desender, K., Beurms, S., & Van den Bussche, E. (2016). Is mental effort exertion contagious? *Psychonomic Bulletin & Review, 23*(2), 624–631.

Doctorow, M., Wittrock, M. C., & Marks, C. (1978). Generative processes in reading comprehension. *Journal of Educational Psychology, 70*(2), 109–118.

Doran, G. T. (1981). There's a S.M.A.R.T. way to write management's goals and objectives. *Management Review, 70*(11), 35–36.

Ericsson, K. A., Krampe, R. T., & Tesch-Romer, C. (1993). The role of deliberate practice in the acquisition of expert performance. *Psychological Review, 100*(3), 363–406.

Ericsson, K. A., & Pool, R. (2016). *Peak: Secrets from the new science of expertise*. Houghton Mifflin Harcourt.

Fiorella, L., & Mayer, R. E. (2015). *Learning as a generative activity: Eight strategies that promote understanding*. Cambridge.

Fiorella, L., & Mayer, R. E. (2016). Eight ways to promote generative learning. *Educational Psychology Review, 28*(4), 717–741.

Fisher, D., & Frey, N. (2018). Let's get jigsaw right. *Educational Leadership, 76*(3), 82–83.

Fisher, D., & Frey, N. (2013). *Better learning through structured teaching: A framework for the gradual release of responsibility* (2nd ed.). ASCD.

Fisher, D., Frey, N., Almarode, J., Flories, K., & Nagel, D. (2020). *PLC+: Better decisions and greater impact by design*. Corwin.

Fisher, D., Frey, N., Hattie, J., & Flores, K. (2019). *Learner's notebook: Becoming an assessment-capable visible learner*. Corwin.

Frey, N., Hattie, J., & Fisher, D. (2018). *Developing assessment-capable visible learners*. Corwin.

Hattie, J. (2012). *Visible learning for teachers: Maximizing impact on learning*. Routledge.

Hattie, J., Fisher, D., Frey, N., Gojak, L. M., Moore, S. D., & Mellman, W. (2017). *Visible learning for mathematics, grades K–12: What works best to optimize student learning*. Corwin.

Kapur, M. (2008). Productive failure. *Cognition and Instruction, 26*(3), 379–424.

Kapur, M. (2014). Productive failure in learning math. *Cognitive Science: A Multidisciplinary Journal, 38*(5), 1008–1022.

The Learning Center, University of North Carolina, Chapel Hill. (n.d.). *Concept maps*. https://learningcenter.unc.edu/tips-and-tools/using-concept-maps

Lorenz, R. (2020). Maunder's work on planetary habitability in 1913: Early use of the term "Habitable Zone" and a "Drake Equation" calculation. *Research Notes of the American Astronomical Society, 4*(6), 79.

Mayer, R. E. (2011). *Applying the science of learning*. Pearson.

McCabe, D. P., & Castel, A. D. (2008). Seeing is believing: The effect of brain images on judgments of scientific reasoning. *Cognition, 107*(1), 343–352.

Medina, J. (2014). *Brain rules: 12 principles for surviving and thriving at work, home and school*. Pear Press.

Merriam-Webster. (2021a). Chance. *Merriam-Webster.com*. https://www.merriam-webster.com/dictionary/chance

Merriam-Webster. (2021b). Design. *Merriam-Webster.com*. https://www.merriam-webster.com/dictionary/design

Merriam-Webster. (2021c). Feedback. *Merriam-Webster.com*. https://www.merriam-webster.com/dictionary/feedback

Merriam-Webster. (2021d). Playbook. *Merriam-Webster.com*. https://www.merriam-webster.com/dictionary/playbook

National Council of Teachers of Mathematics. (2014). *Principles to actions: Ensuring mathematical success for all*. Author.

National Governors Association Center for Best Practices, Council of Chief State School Officers. (2010). *Common core state standards for mathematics*. Author.

NGSS Lead States. (2013). *Next generation science standards: For states, by states*. National Academies Press.

Ormrod, J. E. (2011). *Educational psychology: Developing learners* (7th ed.). Pearson.

Pressley, M., McDaniel, M. A., Turnure, J. E., Wood, E., & Ahmad, M. (1987). Generation and precision of elaboration: Effects on intentional and incidental learning. *Journal of Experimental Psychology, 13*(2), 291–300.

Rickards, F., Hattie, J., & Reid, C. (2021). *The turning point for the teaching profession: Growing expertise and evaluative thinking*. Routledge.

Roediger, H. L., & Karpicke, J. D. (2006). The power of testing memory: Basic research and implications for educational practice. *Perspectives on Psychological Science, 1*(3), 181–210.

Schunk, D. (2019). *Learning theories: An educational perspective* (8th ed.). Pearson.

Seidenberg, M., & Farry-Thorn, M. (2020). *Some context on content. Reading matters. Connecting science and education.* https://seidenbergreading.net/2020/09/10/some-context-on-context/?elementor-preview=3722&ver=1599753685# Footnotes

Simons, D. J., & Chabris, C. F. (1999). Gorillas in our midst: Sustained inattentional blindness for dynamic events. *Perception, 28*(9), 1059–1074.

Smith, M. A., & Karpicke, J. D. (2014). Retrieval practice with short-answer, multiple-choice, and hybrid tests. *Memory, 22*(7), 784–802.

Sweeney, D., & Harris, L. S. (2016). *Student-centered coaching: The moves*. Corwin.

Sweller, J., van Merrienboer, J. J. G., & Paas, F. G. W. C. (1998). Cognitive architecture and instructional design. *Educational Psychology Review, 10*(3), 251–296.

Virginia Department of Education. (2016). *World history and geography to 1500 A.D. (C.E.) history and social science standards of learning*. Author.

Virginia Department of Education. (2020). *Visual arts standard of learning for Virginia public schools*. Author.

Visible Learning Meta[x]. (2021, January). https://www.visiblelearningmetax.com

Index

About the Authors

John Almarode, PhD, is an associate professor and executive director of teaching and learning in the College of Education at James Madison University (JMU). He has worked with schools, classrooms, and teachers all over the world and has presented locally, nationally, and internationally on the application of the science of learning to the classroom, school, and home environments. At JMU, he works with preservice teachers and actively pursues his research interests, including the science of learning and the design and measurement of classroom environments that promote student engagement and learning. John has authored multiple articles, reports, book chapters, and over a dozen books on effective teaching and learning in today's schools and classrooms.

Douglas Fisher, PhD, is Professor of Educational Leadership at San Diego State University and a teacher leader at Health Sciences High. Previously, Doug was an early intervention teacher and elementary school educator. He is the recipient of an International Reading Association William S. Grey citation of merit and an Exemplary Leader award from the Conference on English Leadership of NCTE. He has published numerous articles on teaching and learning as well as books such as *The Teacher Clarity Playbook, PLC+, Visible Learning for Literacy, Comprehension: The Skill, Will, and Thrill of Reading,* and *How Tutoring Works*. Doug loves being an educator and hopes to share that passion with others.

(Continued)

Nancy Frey, PhD, is Professor in Educational Leadership at San Diego State and a teacher leader at Health Sciences High and Middle College. She is a member of the International Literacy Association's Literacy Research Panel. Her published titles include *Visible Learning in Literacy, This Is Balanced Literacy, Removing Labels,* and *Rebound.* Nancy is a credentialed special educator, reading specialist, and administrator in California and learns from teachers and students every day.

CORWIN

A SAGE Publishing Company

> **Every student deserves a great teacher— not by chance, but by design.**

Read more from Fisher & Frey

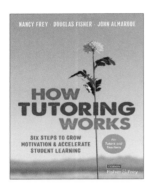

Harnessing decades of Visible Learning® research, this easy-to-read, eye-opening guide details the six essential components of any effective tutoring intervention—establishing a relationship and credibility, addressing student confidence and challenges, setting shared goals, helping a student learn how to learn, teaching and learning content, and establishing a habit of deliberate practice.

Catapult teachers beyond learning intentions to define clearly what success looks like for every student. Designed to be used collaboratively in grade-level, subject-area teams—or even on your own—this step-by-step playbook expands teacher understanding of how success criteria can be utilized to maximize student learning.

Disrupt the cycle of implicit bias and stereotype threat with 40 research-based, teacher-tested techniques; individual, classroom-based, and schoolwide actions; printables; and ready-to-go tools for planning and instruction.

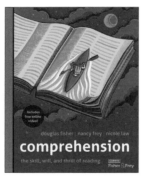

Explore a new model of reading instruction that goes beyond teaching skills to fostering engagement and motivation. *Comprehension* is the structured framework you need to empower students to comprehend text and take action in the world.

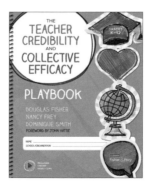

When you increase your credibility with students, student motivation rises. And when you partner with other teachers to achieve this, students learn more. This playbook illuminates the connection between teacher credibility and collective efficacy and offers specific actions educators can take to improve both.

Tap your intuition, collaborate with your peers, and put the research-based strategies embedded in this road map to work in your classroom to implement or deepen a strong, successful balanced literacy program.

To order your copies, visit corwin.com/FisherandFrey